Unstuck

Also by Jane Anne Staw

Parsnips in the Snow

Unstuck

A Supportive and Practical Guide
to Working Through Writer's Block

∾

Jane Anne Staw, Ph.D.

ST. MARTIN'S GRIFFIN ⋈ NEW YORK

www.stmartins.com

Library of Congress Cataloging-in-Publication Data

Staw, Jane Anne
    Unstuck : a supportive and practical guide to working through writer's block / Jane Anne Staw.
        p. cm.
    ISBN 0-312-30120-0 (hc)
    ISBN 0-312-33980-1 (pbk)
    EAN 978-0312-33980-7
    1. Writer's block. 2. Authorship—Psychological aspects. I. Title.

PN171.W74S73 2003
808'.02'019—dc21   2003047133

10 9 8 7 6 5 4 3 2

For Mary, who opened the door for me,
And for Steve, who keeps it open.

Contents

Acknowledgments

First, I want to thank my agent, Victoria Pryor of Arcadia, for being a lifelong friend and the most sensitive and intelligent guide and mentor through the writing and publishing process I could ever imagine. Because of you, from first word to final period, I never felt alone.

Next, I want to thank my editor, Marian Lizzi, for her deep understanding of my book and her bull's-eye suggestions for revision. You are the editor every writer I know fantasizes working with.

Perhaps most important, I want to express my gratitude to all my students and clients over the years. Although I have scrambled your stories and changed names to assure your anonymity, your collective presence fills the pages of this book.

Unstuck

Introduction

For many blocked writers writing is an enemy, not all that different from a growling dog baring its teeth or a stranger sticking a gun to their temple. For others who find it difficult to sit down and write, these images are too dramatic. For them writing is an activity to delay, a chore to postpone. In their minds to associate wolves and guns with writing is hyperbole. More appropriate, they may think, are comparisons to defrosting the freezer or crossing the street to avoid encountering an acquaintance they are not in the mood to meet up with. Perhaps, if they had fewer items on their to-do list, or were feeling more sanguine about their job, or hadn't just had a fight with their partner, they would march to the refrigerator and begin hauling out the frozen food and piling it into the sink. Or they would keep their heads high and greet the acquaintance approaching them, a friendly smile playing on their lips.

As different as these two attitudes toward writing may appear, there is not a great deal of distance between them. No doubt, the first group seems to suffer more. When they are trying to write, they often empty their days of all other obligations, professional, social, and personal. They may worry about what and how they will write long before they begin, their heads spinning with words, half-sentences, and red slashes. They may not be able to sleep. They may lose their appetites. They are indeed miserable, and what's most wrenching is that they are alone in their misery. For no one—not their parents, their partner, their best friend, or their colleagues—can express for them what these tortured writers want to say.

The second group of blocked writers, those who cross the street to avoid the blank screen or page, may appear secure and productive. While they are not writing, their time is filled with activity. Some of them take dance and cooking classes; some begin volunteering at women's shelters and tutorial programs; some pack their days and nights with social encounters, lunches, dinner dates, movies, plays, concerts. Some work longer hours or take an extra job to help pay bills. Some are suddenly inspired to learn French or Italian or Spanish. Or to remodel the kitchen. Or to take up skiing.

But underneath these two different behavior patterns lurks the very same cause: whether writers wring their hands at the prospect of sitting down to write, or remember an important errand just as they turn on their computer, something has soured in the relationship between these writers and their writing. There has been a misunderstanding; someone's feelings have been hurt; one of the parties has misperceived something important about the other's behavior or character. What in particular has gone wrong may be different for each writer. But for now the face of the problem is less important than simply recognizing the dynamic: Whether we write as undergraduates, doctoral candidates, lawyers, accountants, business executives, producers, copywriters, published novelists and poets, or as beginners who have longed to tell our stories for some time but have never found the words, each of us must nurture our relationship with writing, much as we nurture our ties with our partners, our families, and our friends. And just as when something goes wrong in any of these relationships, we must get together with the other party to discuss the problem and explore solutions; when we bump up against writer's block, we must do the same.

In my years leading creative nonfiction workshops, I have come to understand that helping the writers in my classes make their writing world safe is the most important work I can do with them. Writing is a risky business, its terrain full of the land mines of self-criticism and doubt. Thinking about sitting down to write causes many of us to stumble or fall. And not everybody knows how to get up and continue on the path. Instead, many people who desire to write decide that the journey is too dangerous, too filled with risk, to undertake. So they head back home, turning their attention in other directions and leaving the writing behind.

To clear the terrain of land mines and to help my students and clients continue to write, I teach them how best to nurture both themselves as writers and their relationship with their writing. This is as essential as any other instruction I can offer them. Sure, it's helpful if I discuss with them the structure of essays or the role of the narrator in short nonfiction. It's useful to feed them a steady diet of published writing to inspire them and provide models of excellence. And necessary that I offer instructive and positive feedback about their own writing, showing them what they are doing well and suggesting ways to revise what might still need work. But what use is any of this if they aren't writing? Or if they write only sporadically? Or stop writing when the class ends?

Learning your own writing story and attending to your writing process and embracing it are the main ingredients in transforming writing from enemy to friend. My own writing story began when I was an undergraduate at Pembroke College. I was a hand-wringing writer, who suffered over every sentence, over each and every word I wrote. It is a story that begins in darkness and stutters toward the light. The story of a young woman who thought of herself as ordinary—mediocre even. A young woman who felt disenfranchised. Who never, not for one minute, dreamed she might someday become a writer. And certainly a young woman who could not have believed that one day she might help other people write.

It took many years for this story to play itself out. Years of questioning. Of depression. Of frustration. Along the way I experienced moments of breaking through my block, others of crashing into it once again. Moments of keen insight, followed by periods of despair. Parallel to my writing story runs the story of who I am; the plots of these two tales are at times distinct and at other moments twine around each other then merge, the events and epiphanies of one identical to those of the other.

It is through living my own story that I have been able to understand on the most intimate level what it means to be a blocked writer, as well as to understand the journey blocked writers must take to find their way out of the block. Most of what I know comes from observing myself and working with other writers who teach me what I haven't yet learned. Living in Berkeley, California, I know something of psychology. But I have never studied it in any organized way. Nor have I ever approached my work from a clinical point of view. Instead, my approach is empirical. Any theories I have formulated were born from my own experience and the experiences of my clients. Whenever I talk to blocked writers, my primary purpose is to help mend their relationship with writing and, by extension, with themselves. I tell them that we are embarking on a journey together. That I already know parts of the itinerary, but not others. The way I will discover these other destinations and routes is by listening closely to what they, my clients, say, then integrating the tales they tell me with what I have learned works for others who face obstacles to writing. I tell them that this voyage will involve spectacular views and scenery as well as stretches of monotonous freeway. I tell them I will do some of the driving, they the rest. That I will most likely offer pointers on technique. And that I will definitely have something to say about their speed. But if they ask me to tell them where we will end up, I answer, "That I cannot know. Although I promise it will be a much more wonderful place than you could ever imagine. And when you arrive at this destination, you will look back and see that you have been transformed. That without realizing it you have been on a pilgrimage to a personal Lourdes, and that by arriving there you have blessed yourself with the miracle of writing."

When you repair your relationship with writing, your life begins to flow again. Things happen. "When I'm writing, I feel like a magnet," a friend of mine says. "As soon as I pick up my pen, ideas, people, possibilities come my way." At first it might be tiny particles that life shoots toward you. A writer I know who went to journalism school, and who showed great promise that she felt she hadn't lived up to, started writing an essay about her experience as a student and received in the mail an invitation to become a member of her graduate school's alumni board. Waiting for a train to arrive, a client in the middle of a memoir about her childhood ran into her estranged mother for the first time in ten years. Writing about her late and sudden passion for the banjo, another client came across an old photograph of her great-grandmother, playing the very same instrument in a string band. At first each of these events seemed like divine intervention. But as these writers continued to write, they realized that they were responsible for their own miracles. By writing they had awakened to themselves and the world around them, and now they were better able to see what was out there. The woman who had run into her mother at the train stop bumped into her several times after that; she came to understand that her mother had probably been there all along, but the daughter hadn't been looking. The banjo player came to a similar conclusion. Before she began writing about her newfound passion for music, she didn't notice images of music she came upon. And the journalist realized that, during a long period of discouragement over her inability to write, she might well have been throwing away unopened correspondence from her graduate program.

These are the gifts of writing, made possible because, in working so hard to reclaim their right to write, these writers reclaim a part of themselves. You can call what they bring back from their journey their identity or confidence, their voice or passion. You can describe what happens as getting to know—and accept—themselves. As claiming the words to express who they are. As no longer being afraid. These gifts are the creations of energy released when writers are set free to write. Once I was confident that I had worked through my own block, my eyesight for opportunities improved. I could write course descriptions and teach new courses. I could write textbooks. I could give papers at professional meetings. I could write a book about writing block!

Unstuck is a travel guide that will help blocked writers—and writers interested in enriching their relationship with writing in general—undertake this journey. The pages that follow are a road map that can lead troubled writers away from their struggles with writing toward ease and even delight with the act and the process of writing. Along the way you will come upon both specific strategies for facilitating particular turns and vista points that will offer insights into what it takes to put words onto the page. You will find suggestions for ways to sit down and begin to write, for timing writing sessions to fit your anxiety level and attention span, for delineating the writing process into a sequence of discrete phases, and for accumulating positive writing experiences, as well as for selecting your ideal audience and creating a safe writing environment. You will find discussions of the various causes of writing block and of the nature of the relationship between writers and their writing, along with reflections on the efficacy of rewards over punishments in overcoming block, and on the kinds of stories blocked writers tell themselves. Exercises at the end of each chapter offer footholds for integrating what you have read. You might record your responses to these exercises in a journal, and once you finish working your way through the book, you can look back and see how far you've come.

While everyone who reads *Unstuck* will have the same information at their disposal, it is quite likely that no two travelers will follow exactly the same route. For some of you, the answers might lie in strategies as simple as limiting your daily writing time, rewarding yourself after writing sessions, or pretending that what you write—everything from scholarly articles to office memos to chapters of a novel—is a letter to a trusted friend. For others, the trip may involve a more complex itinerary, a combination of behavioral and attitudinal strategies, such as learning to express deep compassion toward yourself as writers or figuring out just what it is you *really* want to write.

All of you will find ways to ease the anxiety of writing, and many will also discover the gifts that writing offers along the way. Most important, once you have read the book, you will find yourself at a destination you could never have anticipated before deciding you'd had enough of remaining silent. Enough of not being able to tell your story. Of not being able to speak your truth on the page. Enough of no longer possessing the right to write.

1

The Right to Write

Every semester, at the first meeting of my creative nonfiction workshop, I ask the students what they hope to gain from the course. There are always a few who say that they are there because they can't write without external pressure. "I need the structure of a class," one student said recently. "I don't write unless I know someone expects me to write and is waiting to receive what I have written," another newcomer confessed. "I can't think of what to write on my own," somebody else admitted.

While these students certainly don't sound like some of the most severely blocked writers I have worked with, anyone who meets up with this much resistance to writing on their own is blocked. Their block may not loom as high as Pike's Peak. It may not even be as substantial as a Sierra foothill. But something lies in the way. An obstacle large enough that they can't scale it or navigate around it arises whenever they think about sitting down at their kitchen table or at the computer in their bedroom or study and trying to write. On their own they are helpless. It is only within the formal structure of the classroom that their words find their way to the page. Set these students on the open highway, and they stall, needing instead the safety of the parking lot where they first learned to drive.

Writing block presents many faces. Blocked writers do not necessarily struggle mightily each time they attempt to collect the words in their heads and form them into phrases, sentences, paragraphs, full pages of text. This is the highest degree of blockage, the near-paralysis of movement—of thoughts, ideas, even single words—from head to hand. It is as if a circuit has been broken, and although energy exists at the point of origin, the pathway for the waves to travel has been destroyed.

This is the face of the block I struggled with in college. When I think of writing as an undergraduate, I see myself alone in the lounge of 99 Brown Street my sophomore year, seated in front of my typewriter, which is set up at a card table I have dragged in from another room of the residence. All around me—in the lounge, on all three floors of the old brown shingle house I live in, in the dormitories on the tiny campus of Pembroke College a block away, as well as in those surrounding the quadrangle at Brown University several blocks farther—it is quiet. Everyone is sleeping. But I am awake. I sit in the tiny lounge, in the skirt and sweater I dressed in that morning before breakfast, the ceiling light glaring down on me. I sit there typing—and retyping—tearing sheet after sheet of paper from the roller, crumpling each one and tossing it onto the pile on the floor beside me, then sliding yet another clean sheet into the platen of my IBM electric typewriter, rolling the carriage until one inch of pristine paper is exposed, then poising my hands above the keyboard and preparing, once again, to type.

I am trying to finish a paper due the next day. The subject of the paper doesn't matter. I might be writing an essay for my Chinese history class or a term paper for a class in religion. I might have something to turn in for philosophy or sociology. For archaeology. For psychology. And it doesn't have to be my sophomore year. It could be as early as my freshman year. Or as late as the end of my junior year, when I became passionate about the history of religions and took a sequence of courses on the Old and New Testaments and then on Hinduism and Buddhism.

Despite appearances, I have not waited until the last minute to begin writing this paper. No matter when the professor assigned it—a month, two months, before its due date—I set to work immediately, researching, outlining, researching again. Writing a thesis statement. Then another. And another. Sitting down to put actual words on paper. Typing in the first sentence. Stopping. Reading it aloud. Frowning. Pulling the page out and inserting another. Typing yet another first sentence, one or two words at a time, reading the sentence from the beginning each time I stop to think, to search for a word, an expression, a spelling. This time I might complete the first sentence and move on to the next. But I will inevitably stop mid-second-sentence and yank the paper out of the typewriter, throwing it in the general direction of the first. By the end of several hours, perhaps I will have one intact paragraph.

And so it will be, each time I sit down to work on this paper, for five days in a row, or for three weeks or a month or two months. And the day before the paper is due, I will still be writing, not just to the end, toward my summary and my conclusion, away from the tension and indecision of the first words, but once again from the beginning. Yes, from the beginning. For each time I write I take it from the top, refining what I have already written, word by word, sentence by sentence until the early paragraphs— and often more, much more—are as ornate as a Fabergé egg.

Luckily, most blocked writers do not suffer to this degree. For many the pathway between head and hand exists but is no longer intact. Or the signals encounter interference as they travel out-

ward. As a consequence, their words come slowly and with difficulty. Or the sentences do not flow, one from the other. Or what
appears upon the page is not at all what the writers meant to say
or even thought they were saying. These damaged pathways create their fair share of unhappiness and frustration. And it's not
difficult to imagine how the unhappiness and frustration might
escalate over time. After all, not only do these writers experience
no reward in writing; each time they write, they are left with an
unpleasant aftertaste.

"Can you help me say what I'm trying to say?" a prospective
client asked me on the phone the other day. "I mean, I don't seem
to have trouble *writing*. I sit down and the words flow. But my
writing never turns out the way I want it to." Another client, who
made an appointment because she wanted to work on her style,
arrived for our first meeting and announced, "The truth is, it
takes me much too long to write. And I don't just mean important documents. You should see how many drafts I compose of a
silly thank-you note!"

Other writers, with no history of difficulty, find themselves
blocked for the first time the last semester of their senior year in
college. Or in the middle of writing their dissertation. Or their
first tenure article. I once worked with a university professor who
had accumulated quite a bibliography of academic publications.
Then he decided to try something different. He wanted to write
a more personal piece. Not a completely personal piece. But an
essay that combined his research with observations and stories
from his life. And he found himself mute! Here he was, a full professor known for his eloquence, his curriculum vitae studded
with awards and laurels, and he couldn't write a word.

Or what about the stay-at-home mother who received praise

for her writing throughout college, and who desired to write a short story she had carried in her head for years but never seemed to get around to actually writing it down? By the time I met her, she was furious at herself. "After all, I should be able to set aside an hour a day to write. I'm lucky enough not to have to work, and I don't have all that many obligations. And my God, my kids are in school all day. What's wrong with me?"

The most elusive of writing blocks masquerades as writing to deadline. We all know people who wait until the night before a term paper, a legal brief, a business report is due to sit down and begin writing. If asked, most of these writers would claim, "I write best if I wait until the last minute." Most people who write to deadline don't realize they are blocked—until they face a writing project that simply can't be completed the night before it is due. For a long time I thought that journalism nurtured this adrenaline-filled, roller-coaster relationship with writing. After all, you can only write about news once it has broken. Then I became a member of a writing group that included a journalist who had moved from news to feature stories, and no matter what her topic or how far in advance she received the assignment, she continued to write to deadline. With disastrous results. Watching this woman panic about not being able to finish each piece that was due, I realized that my logic might have been backward. Newswriting doesn't *necessarily* nurture writing to deadline; instead, it might attract writers who are most comfortable waiting until the last possible minute.

I'd probably be safe in claiming that at least 25 percent of the students in my workshop classes write to deadline. "I love writing, and I want to write. But I don't seem to get anything done unless I'm faced with a deadline," one might say. Or, "I always turn in my assignments. The problem is, I don't get to them until the midnight before they are due." While these last-minute writers seem at first to have a lot in common with the writers who need structure and assignments to write, over the years I have discovered an important difference between the two. Deadline writers don't usually blame themselves for not getting around to writing; they blame their schedules or their jobs or the other people in their lives. "I know I have to eliminate one or two of my activities if I want to write, but I can't seem to figure out what to drop," a writer told me last semester. Another student asked the class to help her figure out how to say no to at least part of her social life. "My friends don't seem to understand when I tell them I want to stay home and write," she said. Many of my clients struggle over the writing-versus-exercise competition. "I don't have time to do both," they tell me. "And the trouble is, I feel rotten when I don't exercise and rotten when I don't write."

No matter what stories they tell about not being able to write, and no matter how convincing their stories are, all of these writers struggle with writer's block, though its face might look different to each of them. It may scowl at the client who disliked how his writing turned out, glare at the woman who labored over her thank-you notes, grimace at the blocked university professor. It may hoot or boo at other writers. Or it may laugh raucously every time they put a word on the page. It is not through its appearance that I diagnose writer's block, but through the way it interferes with people's lives. Whether they agonize in order to write or chronically hesitate to put words on paper, whether they avoid writing whenever they possibly can or hate whatever they do write, anybody whose relationship with writing is impaired suffers from some degree of blockage.

Think about how we all would suffer if we struggled to the

same extent and degree with speaking. Some of us would remain mute. We'd watch life as it played itself out before us. And as we watched, we'd think; sometimes our thoughts would even be profound. But we would hardly say a word. Others of us would hesitate a good while before we opened our mouths, worrying about how to express what we were thinking, what words to use, how quickly or slowly to speak, what intonation to settle upon. And when we did speak, we might become flustered, contradicting ourselves immediately. Taking back what we said. Apologizing for ourselves. "That's not really what I meant to say. I didn't use the right words. I spoke too quickly. Let me try again. No, that's not right either. It's more that I. . . ."

Of course, what I'm describing will strike you as ridiculous. After all, most of us do enjoy the power of speech, a power that was cultivated lovingly by our parents as soon as we pronounced our first word. It's true that some of our mothers corrected our grammar, particularly once we entered high school. Mine wanted me to answer the phone by saying, "It is I," if anyone asked to speak with Jane Anne. I even occasionally slip in a correction, in the form of an innocent restatement, when my son, Jonah, speaks. But Jonah is twenty-eight and for at least his first ten years, I listened adoringly to everything he said.

These are not at all the conditions most of us experienced around our writing. Beginning in kindergarten, the way we formed our letters and our words was scrutinized and corrected by our teachers—and often by our parents as well. There was a prescribed way to hold the pencil, to move it across the page, to create each letter, both uppercase and lowercase. And just when we thought we were able to write, we entered third grade and were told that printing didn't count; we now had to learn cursive. So many more opportunities to misform our letters, to slant our writing in the wrong direction, to misconnect or disconnect. To do it wrong.

It is no wonder that so many of us struggle with writing block in its various forms. Only the staunchest of us could march through the minefields of cursive and sentences and grammar and diagramming and paragraphs and essays without being wounded. Complicate these smaller injuries with the assault of a teacher who tears up our wrinkled piece of lined paper and tells us to start again. Or the teacher who tells us that what we have written makes no sense. That our spelling makes us look stupid. Or a parent who tells us he or she is embarrassed to read what we have written. Or asks if that is the best we can do.

In America we believe in our right to say what we think. If someone feels they have been punished for or intimidated about speaking his or her mind, they can demand their First Amendment rights. If they have not been allowed to speak, they can claim freedom of speech. In Berkeley every teenager knows about Mario Savio and the Free Speech Movement. About how the students took over the administration building at the university in order to make themselves heard.

As someone whose ability to express herself on the page was nearly silenced, I am equally passionate about our right to write. I don't mean writing poetry or oratory, novels or treatises. I mean writing what we think, what we desire and hope for, what we love and what we hate. I mean telling our stories on the page, or the stories of our families. I mean arguing with written words for a cause we believe in or against a cause somebody else believes in. I mean writing about our summer vacation. About the foods we love. The games we play.

In the course of working my way through my own serious writing block, I remembered that as a kid I had written poetry. I don't know when I composed my first verses, but in seventh grade I won a literary contest, and my poem "Autumn Leaves" was published in a slim anthology. Three years later, at the beginning of high school, I was still writing poetry. This time, my ninth-grade English teacher recognized my talent, and once again one of my poems was published. Four years later, sitting in my dorm room at college, I could no longer write. What had happened? What mine had exploded, hurling its shrapnel on the part of me that had composed those tender poems? Or if it wasn't as violent an event as a mine exploding, what collection of injuries—of cuts and scrapes, bumps and bruises, twisted muscles and broken bones—had I acquired between ninth grade and my freshman year in college? What scabs and scars were inhibiting my writing, making it almost too painful to write? Who or what in those four years had revoked my right to write?

It took me fifteen years years to stand up for my rights, to begin putting words on the page again, and to allow those words to accumulate, slowly, into poems, essays, and stories. And now, for all those who have lost this right, I'm evangelical about reclaiming it. Now is the time. Writing is the way. I use the classroom and my office as a pulpit. I preach at dinner parties. On the telephone. On walks with friends. I want everyone to see the light, to know that they can relieve themselves of the misery of not writing, of the frustration of not liking what they write, of the fear of not being able to write at all. And I offer to show blocked writers they can do this. Not by looking for culprits. And not by filling themselves with regret or thinking of all the time they have wasted. I want to help by assisting them in the process of recovery. By showing them that their struggle or their strain with writing, while personal and particular, also shares a great deal with the struggles and strains of many other people who find it uncomfortable to write. That by recognizing their responses and reactions, understanding their origins and motivations, and learning new strategies to deal with writing, blocked writers can reclaim their right to write, just as I did.

Try This

1. Think about sitting down to write—a report, a term paper, a legal brief, a short story, or any other form you choose—and observe your emotions, your thoughts, and your physical response. Do you feel a sense of dread? Does your heart beat faster? Do you tell yourself, "This will never work out"? Or do you quickly think of something else you should be doing instead?

2. If you have caught yourself avoiding writing or feeling tense about it, ask yourself why. Ask yourself, "Why do I always wait to begin until the writing is due the next day? Why have I suddenly decided to learn Spanish or train for a marathon? Why do I find time to solve everybody else's problems but not to do my writing?"

3. If the topic of writing comes up in conversation, how do you react? Do you join right in? Or do you stop participating? Do you try to change the topic? Walk away?

4. What have you done to encourage—or force—yourself to write? Have you felt angry with yourself for not writing? Punitive?

5. Think about sitting down to write. What images arise for you?

6. If you usually write to deadline, try beginning your next writing project ahead of time. Notice how you feel writing in advance. What kinds of thoughts run through your head?

2

When It All Began

I don't know exactly when or why my writing block began. I wasn't tormented by term papers in high school, although, as I recall, my teachers were more enthusiastic in their support of my class participation than of my written work. Yet I joined the high-school newspaper, the *Merionite,* and I even garnered a reputation for the articles I wrote. In fact, I won an award from Columbia University as an outstanding high-school journalist.

So what went wrong?

What went wrong, indeed! How could I have traveled so far from my experience as a journalist in such a short time? How could I have so quickly exchanged the exhilaration of being honored for my writing at a public assembly for the panic of incompetence I suffered each time I sat down to write?

What soon comes to mind is a scene between my father and me in the fall of my senior year in high school. I am writing my application for early admission to Pembroke College. I have worked long and hard on the personal essay, which I have just completed, and my father is sitting in my bedroom at my desk, reading my draft. When he finishes reading and puts the paper down, what I remember is his turning to me and shaking his head sadly. "This will never do," he tells me. "It will never do. We'll have to write it all over again!"

Now, I am not saying that these were my father's words. I am saying that these are the words I *remember*. My father may well have said something different. He may have only suggested that the essay needed work. Or he may have said nothing at all. He may merely have picked up his pencil and begun revising. But whatever he said and whatever his actions, I understood what I understood: My essay was a failure.

I remember something else as well. I remember that I felt as if all the air had been squeezed out of me. The room went dark. All sound was muffled. I don't know if this was because I felt humiliated at having failed in the eyes of my father, whom I revered, at something as important as this essay. Or because I suddenly realized that I might not be accepted at Pembroke, that I might not be good enough.

I don't remember much of the rest of the evening. I no longer even recall what my revised essay was about, although I'm certain I played up my experience speaking French in hopes of distinguishing myself from the scores of other applicants. I do know that I was denied an early decision but was accepted for general admission in the spring, along with the rest of the future freshman class. And I know that, by the time I arrived on campus, or at least by the time my first paper was due, I could no longer write.

I am not saying that my father, by criticizing my essay, was responsible for my writing block. I am not implying anything of the sort. I am merely remembering events and attempting to reconstruct my life as a blocked writer. None of this is science. The incidents are not verifiable. If I asked my father, or even my mother, what happened when I had finished a draft of my college essay, I'm certain each would have something different to say. My mother would most likely defer to my father: "I didn't have much to do with that," she would probably respond. "I'm sure Daddy helped you. After all, he was the writing expert." As for my father,

I can't imagine that he would remember that particular interaction at all.

No, this is not science. It is memory and emotion. It is story. And the story of my father's response to my college essay is a story I may have been telling myself for years without being aware of it. For if anyone had asked me why I had so much trouble writing when I was in college, I am almost certain I would not have pointed to the interaction with my father over my application essay. I would more likely have responded with a tautology: I had trouble writing because I wrote poorly.

In the years I have been working with blocked writers, it has been rare for anyone to isolate a single determining event, or even a series of events, as causing their block. When they first come to see me most people put the blame squarely on themselves, telling me they aren't writing their dissertation or their legal briefs because they can't organize their thoughts or their time, they lack sufficient motivation, they are distracted by the piles of papers on their desks, or they have too many other obligations.

No one who was or is having difficulty sitting down to write has said to me, "I can't write my history term paper because my mother criticized a story I wrote in the fourth grade." Or, "My year-end report is a week late because my high-school English teacher gave me an F on my analysis of *Hamlet*."

I once worked with a woman, a law student, who told me that her father frequently forced her and her siblings to stay up the whole night writing. He would set them up at the dining room table, announce a topic, and tell them they couldn't stop until he gave them permission to go to bed. Often he kept their hands moving across the page until dawn. But this was not one single event or moment. It was chronic and constant trauma, repeated over years. And in spite of this cruelty my client had made it all the way through her second year of law school before she felt too terrified to write.

Another writer came to me because, each time he tried to write, the image of an elementary-school teacher striding between rows of desks, wearing combat boots and brandishing a stick, came to mind and wouldn't leave, filling him with terror. My client couldn't understand why this image came over him when he wrote, since he had not begun writing until high school. This man was sick with AIDS and was writing his memoirs, and he gradually realized that it wasn't the act of writing that filled him with fear; rather, it was the isolation and disapproval he had experienced as a young boy who never fit in that still terrified him. The teacher in combat boots embodied that disapproval.

If my father's reaction to my college essay contributed to or fueled my writing block, it was because the soil in my psyche was fertile enough for this incident to develop roots and take hold. And my keen memory of the event means only that the tree it grew into was hefty. In the same way, the soil into which the journalism award was planted was deficient; the scrub that grew from it, easy to overlook. And just as any soil a gardener plants season after season needs nutrients to maintain its fertility, any doubt I entertained about my ability to write was thoroughly fertilized by the comments and corrections riddling every term paper my professors in college returned to me: "These sentences are unwieldy." "What are you trying to say here?" "Good idea, poor expression." "You cram too many ideas into every sentence." "This sentence is incomprehensible." These reactions reinforced the doubt I had about myself as a writer, so that soon I could not help but think of my professors' criticisms every time I sat down to write.

Oddly, though, despite this continuing criticism writing during college did not become increasingly difficult for me. The pain I experienced whenever I had a paper due was firmly in place by the second semester of my freshman year, and it pursued me with more or less the same intensity all four years. But my story is not typical. Most writers who come to see me have experienced increasing difficulty with writing over a period of years. For many the problem began with procrastination. Instead of sitting easily down to write a term paper, a memo, even a thank-you note, they *think* about getting to work for longer and longer periods of time before they actually do it. Most of them rely on deadlines for motivation. Then one day these writers discover that even with a deadline looming they can no longer force themselves to begin. After years of adrenaline-filled hours in front of their typewriters or computers, some of them can no longer even pick up a pen to jot a note to a friend or colleague.

As we work together, blocked writers often gradually remember negative experiences surrounding their writing. Many recall a parent who disapproved of the way they wrote. Others once again feel the sting of a teacher's criticism. One client remembered the long-forgotten red slashes a high-school English teacher scrawled all over her papers. Still another realized that she had always associated writing with her novelist father, who was highly critical of her while she was growing up. While they were writing to deadline, even when they became aware of procrastinating, none of these writers was conscious of the associations they carried with them. It was only once we explored their writing history together that these memories surfaced.

While some writers are aware of their procrastination, aware of constantly telling themselves, "I'll write it later," others are not conscious of their chronic delay. Instead of thinking about the writing they ought to be doing, these writers push it out of their minds by busying themselves with appointments, financial-planning seminars, personal trainers, lunch dates, soccer coaching, computer classes, dinner parties—even writing courses—so they literally don't have time for thoughts of the academic or work-related writing they should attend to. In order to keep themselves safe from the blank page or computer screen, they make certain they always have something else to do, an "obligation" that allows them to turn their backs on the writing they *should* be doing. And if their Palm Pilots fail to keep them busy enough, they engage themselves at home. They scour their houses, organize their files, paint their dining rooms, landscape their parking strips, refinish their kitchen tables. These may be worthwhile endeavors, but, when they are motivated by discomfort around writing, we need to rethink our schedules.

Often it is difficult for blocked writers to see that they are using busyness to keep anxiety around writing at bay. "Isn't exercise important?" several clients have recently asked me. "I don't think I can concentrate on my writing until I know my retirement is secure," another client, divorced for several years, told me. "My mother has always wanted me to help her organize her photo albums," yet another writer said. "And I've just realized that she's getting old, so I'd better not put this off any longer, or I'm afraid I may be sorry."

"Of course exercise is important," I answer. "But haven't you just increased the number of yoga classes or training sessions or extended your running schedule?" "I too was divorced and concerned about my financial future, so I understand the importance of retirement planning, but why does this exclude writing?" "I have been promising myself that I would create order out of the chaos of the photographs I've taken over the past ten years. But why put a photograph album before your writing?"

What I suggest to writers who come down with a case of hyperscheduling is that they ask themselves a simple question: Why now? Why, just when I was about to begin writing my book or my article or my dissertation, have I decided to substantially increase my exercise or embark on a project I have been considering on and off for a long time? Is my motive truly to work toward better health? To plan judiciously for my retirement? To spend time with my mother? Or are these excuses, diversions, means toward a more oblique end? Is it possible that, like Aesop's fox, I am a master of distraction? Do I sincerely want to accomplish this new task, or am I using it to keep me from thinking about the writing I was planning to do? Am I keeping myself busy to avoid sitting down to write?

Once writers are able to look at their busy schedules with a clearer eye and to entertain the possibility that their busyness is a strategy—often not a conscious one—to keep them "safe" from writing, they are ready to begin wondering why. *Why is it so difficult for me to sit down to write? Why do I want to avoid writing so desperately that I schedule myself ragged? Why am I always running around taking care of everybody else—my mother, my best friend, my next-door neighbor?*

The first whys to surface often revolve around damaging experiences related to writing or self-expression. Often these involve negative interactions about writing in school. And if the soil is rich, these experiences tend to take root, leading to subsequent failures. One of my clients experienced a dramatic trigger when she became seriously ill right after she turned in her master's thesis. Despite years of therapy and a deep and broad understanding of what had taken place—and why—this client continued to associate writing, or completing an important document, with physical collapse, and although she attended law school and was recruited to teach at a prestigious law school, she found herself unable to begin work on the articles necessary to earn her tenure. Prior to college writing had been a source of solace for her, but after her breakdown writing conjured only loss.

I have seen over the years that one negative writing experience can, for some writers, set the dominoes in motion to cancel a life-time of writing comfort. We are extremely vulnerable around our writing—so vulnerable that any negative event, no matter how small or how early, may begin the avalanche, eventually burying us in fear. One client recalled an episode in fourth grade when her teacher held up a sample of her handwriting to the class for ridicule; she realized that was when her struggle with writing had actually begun. Subsequent difficulty, most likely ripples of that experience, eventually made the waters too troubled for her to write, and she dropped out of college. When she came to see me, she had decided she wanted to conquer her block and complete her BA. Another client remembered being humiliated in elemen-tary school when his teacher read his vacation essay aloud at the beginning of the school year. What his family had done that sum-mer was out of the ordinary, and my client had been embarassed at having his vacation made public. After that, he associated writ-ing with embarassment. An African-American client of mine realized that his seventh-grade English teacher had silenced him by circling in red each nonstandard English usage in every paper he turned in, making him fear that each time he wrote he might inadvertently reveal something shameful about his background. He kept writing despite his anxiety until he was a partner in a prestigious law firm and he found that no amount of willpower could make him sit down and write.

This deeply personal shame and rejection—whether intended

or not—is what makes these early writing experiences so lasting. In my case, I'd had my heart set on attending Pembroke, and I viewed my application essay as an intimate portrait of who I was. What I took away from my father's response was that who I was wasn't good enough. His perceived criticism struck hard and deep. The wound was formed, and each subsequent response to my writing made it bleed again, until just to think about writing hurt.

If I never became a completely blocked writer and remained instead a tormented one, it is because I majored in French. I now see that, without this second language that allowed me to exist independently from my blocked self, my college education quite likely would have come to a halt sometime during my sophomore or junior year. Writing term papers for three or four courses in English each semester would have pushed me to a point of mental and emotional exhaustion. Taking weeks to complete each of several papers for four courses, I would simply have run out of time. And if the only feedback I received about my writing was negative, I would have run out of confidence and courage as well. Without the wings of French I well might have reached the impasse of one of my clients. She had gotten married a year earlier and had still not been able to write thank-you notes for the gifts she and her husband had received. Not only was she personally tormented by her silence—she feared that all the guests by now considered her ungrateful and selfish—her parents were upset on the part of all of their friends whose generosity had gone unacknowledged. Her parents were so troubled that they canceled their Thanksgiving trip to her new home to give her time to write her notes. "That way, you won't have any more excuses. You can just sit down and do it," her father told her. By the time she came to see me, my client was distraught. "Not only is this writing thing ruining my life," she wailed, "it's hurting my parents and interfering with my marriage."

French was my sanctuary. My writing block remained contained, activated only when I had to write in English. If we associate writing with negative experiences in the past, consciously or unconsciously these associations arise each time we sit down to write, and we become solidly conditioned *against* writing. After a while our responses to the conditioned stimulus become automatic and unknowing, increasingly reinforced over time and repeated exposures to the blank page.

By making their first appointment with me, either because their writing situation has become desperate or because they are tired of living with their handicap, my clients are taking the first step in breaking a chain that has been choking them for longer than they care to remember.

Whatever we do to overcome a writing block, it should involve taking a direction in which we have not headed before. Doing more of the same—avoiding, criticizing, blaming, beating up on ourselves—is certain to lead to failure. Hope often lies in taking a different route, or at least an unexpected turn. I once had a friend who was constantly in search of adventure. She decided that one way to encounter it was to invent new routes for traveling to work in the morning. It took her about a half hour to arrive at her job, and at the end of each month, she studied a local map to discover a new twist or turn that would renew her journey. She found that the change kept her refreshed, invigorating her to approach both her workplace and her profession with more enthusiasm. The scenery along her drive never became stale, and the monthly newness allowed her to engage in the day's tasks with an open and more creative mind.

Interrupting our habitual series of behaviors and responses

toward writing gives us a chance to open ourselves to new reactions and attitudes. We might interrupt our usual negative thoughts when we sit down to write by reassuring ourselves that we can rehabilitate our relationship with writing. Or congratulate ourselves for taking the first step toward overcoming our block. By changing our approach, either dramatically or in small measures, we may make what was once inevitable disappear, so that one day we will find ourselves at a new and more positive destination. Each of us must find our own way to this destination, our route a combination of strategies and approaches tailored to our particular needs, idiosyncrasies, and comfort levels. What matters is not the particular route we discover, but that, whatever twists and turns, highways and backroads, we follow, it is possible for each of us to land in the same place: a spot where writing is no longer a struggle.

Try This

1. Imagine yourself writing in third grade, or in seventh. How about in high school? In college? How does it feel to be writing at each of these times? Do you remember a time when writing was a pleasant experience?

2. If you are able to recall any pleasant writing experiences, make a note of them. Then remind yourself of these experiences whenever you think about writing.

3. If you have been able to recognize a time when the seas parted, a time before writing became difficult and a time after, can you remember any experiences around this time that might have contributed to your block?

4. Once you have pinpointed an experience, or several, you might ask yourself, "Did that really happen in exactly the way I remember? Or does my memory consist of a large dose of interpretation on my part?"

5. If you have been able to isolate experiences that have contributed to your block, you might begin repeating to yourself, "My difficulties with writing are not my fault, and now I am working to overcome them."

3

Flushing Out Our Enemies

"I never realized I was so lazy," a young woman in one of my summer workshops piped up at the beginning of class one evening. "I used to run at least seven miles a day and work out at the gym five nights a week, but now I can't get myself to sit down in front of my computer and write."

"Me too," another young women chorused. "Just two years ago, when I was in college, I could exercise, study, and party till two in the morning, and I could always get out of bed the minute my alarm rang. Now, no matter how much I promise myself that I'll sit down and write once I get home from work, I can't seem to make it happen. I've become a total sloth."

Energetic, slender, their skin glowing with health and vitality, these two women look anything but lazy. In fact, anyone listening to them would probably assume that they were joking. Anyone except me. I know they mean what they say. I know because I have heard this before, in class and in private consultations with blocked writers. I've heard it from men and women, from recent graduates of prestigious universities, from doctoral students who have passed their preliminary exams and presented papers at professional meetings, from attorneys who have been practicing law successfully for a number of years or teaching in major law schools.

I've heard this, and I've heard much more—everything from

"I'm lazy" to "I'm just no good." From "I'm undisciplined" to "I'm unworthy." From "I need a push" to "I need you to yell at me." Or, "I need you to remind me that I'm throwing twenty years of education down the drain." "Tell me what a failure I am."

It's astonishing how quickly writers turn against themselves. Once we have trouble sitting down to write for several sessions, the jury of voices inside our heads quickly reaches a verdict. "Guilty," the foreman announces early on week three or four. "Guilty of laziness, sloth, lack of discipline, weak will, lack of focus." And if that severe verdict isn't enough, the presiding judge follows the announcement by sentencing the guilty party to years, perhaps a lifetime, of self-criticism. Then, as the blocked writer slinks out of the courtroom, all those present—teachers, parents, bosses, mentors, even friends—point their fingers and jeer: "Failure!" "No good!" "You ought to be ashamed!"

Exposure to so much self-abuse from the writers I teach and those I work with has taught me to see writing block as a kind of autoimmune disease, a condition that causes people to turn against themselves and become their own harshest, most relentless critics. It is as if we have spent years gathering an arsenal of weapons that we keep at hand to one day aim, point-blank, at ourselves. Harsh words about our writing from teachers. Criticism from parents. Societal norms that beatify self-discipline and willpower. A culture where strategies for self-improvement proliferate.

American mythology is full of stories about self-made men like Abraham Lincoln, Andrew Carnegie, and Warren Buffett, who as a child went door-to-door selling soda pop to raise money for his future. Interviews with Lance Armstrong, before and after the Tour de France; with writers like Stephen Covey, who not only has written seven books but knows the essential habits for success; with politicians like Bill Clinton, whose race for the presidency began years before he actually ran, at a tiny farmhouse in rural Arkansas. Writers hoard this arsenal of recriminatory examples. Then as soon as the writing stops, the minute words refuse to make the journey from their heads onto the page, writers reach into the arsenal and begin firing.

A culture where the Protestant work ethic and a fervent belief in the power of will and reason walk hand in hand is to a great extent responsible. Collectively, we believe in the absolute goodness of hard work, and, by extension, that hard work inevitably yields positive results. If as writers we can't produce, the reason *must* be a lack of hard work on our part. We must be lazy—that's all there is to it. Or if "hard work" seems too reductive, we can move ahead several centuries beyond the Pilgrims to the modern era, when we repositioned our altars, setting them this time in front of reason and willpower, believing that to accomplish anything, even good health, we need simply focus our minds on the object of our desire. "If I really wanted to write, I would be writing," a client with a severe block told me not long ago. "I must not care all that much." The distance between a statement like this and self-condemnation concerning our moral defects—*I'm lazy, weak, a failure, don't deserve to graduate, to get tenure, earn money*—is much too short. Again and again I've seen it happen: If writers don't manifest the results of hard work, they conclude that they have failed to apply their will to writing. And because they are lacking in willpower, they figure they deserve the litany of blame and shame they hurl at themselves.

You might think that, having heard the barrage of self-criticism and condemnation so often, I would have become inured to it by now. That I would not notice the nastiness my clients direct at themselves any more than I take in mundane comments about the weather. But just the opposite has happened.

I've become highly sensitized to the destructive ways blocked writers refer to themselves. I flinch as soon as the words "What I need" tumble out of a writer's mouth. I know what is coming, and I want to stop the sentence in midstream, want to keep the self-hate and blame from filling the air. "No, don't!" I react quickly. "Whatever you were about to say, don't say it."

"I was just going to say that what I need is a good. . . ."

"Stop!" I command. "Nobody in my workshops [or in my office] is allowed to be mean to himself or herself. That's one of my core rules."

I am not naive. I know that simply ordering blocked writers to stop hurling invectives their own way won't change what they're thinking or feeling. Of course not. It takes a great deal of work and often many months to affect the way writers react to their difficulty with writing. Overcoming writing block takes time. Telling writers not to be mean to themselves is simply a first step. A first step that fulfills *two* functions simultaneously: It is the first swing of the wrecking ball in dismantling the very bad habit of self-criticism. At the same time it is the first lesson in self-kindness: "Don't say mean things about yourself out loud—and certainly not in front of anybody else."

"But why should I be nice to myself?" most blocked writers will ask. "I'm screwing up. I'm supposed to write this magazine article, and I'm not doing it. I deserve to be punished."

In the beginning I have to say, "Trust me when I tell you that it is only through practicing self-kindness that you will be able to write again—whether you have been blocked for years or only for a matter of weeks." Once I have succeeded in stanching the flow of self-blame, I begin to make my case. "Do you know any adults who are motivated by punishment?" I ask. "Mature men and women who inspire themselves successfully by applying the whip? Come on," I challenge, "name someone you know who jogs, plays the piano, writes novels, practices yoga, swims, enters tennis tournaments—for an extended period of time—because they tell themselves they are rotten and no good if they do not."

The writers I work with have to agree that everybody they know who engages in any of the above activities does so out of passion. Because of the joy or sense of accomplishment they derive from whatever they are doing—be it playing a Beethoven sonata or running a marathon. But very quickly my clients raise a finger and tell me that writing is different. Those activities are all optional. For a good part of our life writing is not.

True enough. But that's not the truth I'm trying to help writers to see. What I want them to understand is that the best motivation, the most effective incentive, for any activity is some form of positive reinforcement. And since we are embarking on a process aimed at helping blocked writers begin to write again, it not only makes sense, it is also in their best interest to use the most powerful tools at hand. Positive reinforcement is one of those tools.

For any skeptics I can cite data—drawn from research conducted by psychologists trained in experimental methods—that establish the efficacy of positive reinforcement and its superiority over punishment or negative reinforcement. But I usually don't need to. Instead, I appeal to common sense. Think about it. Most of us do what we are drawn to and avoid what we dislike. If we have trouble writing or even sitting down to write, it is quite likely that *something* about writing or the act of writing—perhaps even about the consequences of writing—is unappealing. Otherwise, we would not be blocked. It's that simple. Attributes like laziness, lack of motivation, and disorganization are most often ways of describing a more basic reaction. Because working at our desks or our computers feels bad, we avoid them. We allow our papers to pile up and the piles to topple over. We leave our thank-you notes blank. Our term papers and novels unwritten. Our legal briefs aborted midway. But we are certainly not lazy. Far from it. Our lives are a flurry of activity. At home we arrange our cookbooks and CD collections on our library shelves. We clear out our closets. We stop off at the gym on our way home from work, and we never miss a rehearsal for the community theater production we are part of. Anything to keep us from thinking about the writing we are avoiding. Because something about working at our desks feels bad, we allow our papers to pile up and the piles to topple over.

My first line of reasoning for convincing writers to stop punishing themselves is practicality. It's simply impractical to beat ourselves up for not writing. It doesn't work. So, for the sake of efficiency, try stopping. No need to believe what I am telling you. Belief will arise later, once you see that my approach works.

This appeal to efficiency is attractive to writers who feel that they have wasted large amounts of time not writing, and that as a consequence they have fallen far behind in the work they want to do. I'm quick to warn that I'm speaking about efficiency, not speed. Overcoming writing block takes time. But if you stop chastising yourself, you've taken the first and perhaps the most important step.

For many blocked writers name-calling has become such an ingrained habit, they have difficulty catching themselves in the act. Or they truly believe that they could use a kick in the butt or that it would help if I yelled at them, and they are unaware of the degree or extent of their self-directed cruelty. Part of the reason for their lack of awareness is that a lot of the name-calling is not conscious. They may know that they think they are lazy or sloppy or not motivated. But they don't know—are unable to hear—the litany of self-abuse they practice outside of awareness.

For the first weeks or months of working through writing block, I suggest that writers record any thoughts they have about themselves or their writing as they try to write. If they're using a computer, I suggest perhaps opening two windows simultaneously. If they are writing longhand, I suggest laying two sheets of paper side by side. Whether you are writing your dissertation, a legal brief, a departmental memo, or a thank-you note, it's important to remain conscious of the white noise in your head and to capture that noise on the screen or on the page.

After I suggest this to my clients, it is not unusual for them to come back to me the very next week with a sentence or two of the text they intended to write, and pages of background noise. In fact, whenever writers return with just a few notations of mild self-abuse, I suspect censorship, and I have them repeat the exercise immediately, in my office, in hopes of catching the censors off guard. Most of the time writers are surprised by both the volume *and* the intensity of their self-criticism. Even though I have alerted them, they are never prepared for just how cruel they are to themselves. "You're just a piece of crap, and you don't deserve to be paid for any of the work you do." "You're too stupid to know how to spell, and you're even stupider to think you can learn to write. Give it up!" "You're fat and ugly, and everybody hates you." "Your mother was right. You're a bitch and a failure." "Don't even bother writing that brief. You may have fooled your law professors, but you're not going to fool the judge. He's going to laugh at you, and so will the jury. Every single member!"

It's painful to listen to the abuse blocked writers fling at themselves. Many times, after my clients have read out loud what they have recorded, we remain quiet for a long time, near tears not only at the cruelty of teachers and parents but at the longevity of their words and the permanence of the damage they have done.

But I don't suggest this exercise out of cruelty. Rather, this awareness is useful on many fronts: By creating this record you become acquainted with the enemy. The voices you hear usually belong to people you know or have known—people who, because of their relationship to you, have been able to inject the poison of self-doubt deep into your psyche. Once you can attach a name and a face to each voice, you come to know your enemies and realize that many of the voices you hear are not your own but those of a depressed parent, a frustrated teacher, a hostile boss, a jealous sibling. Now you can begin to take the insults and criticisms less personally and strategize on how best to respond.

One client began to wonder if his mother's hawkish correction of the punctuation and grammar in his writing was motivated by her embarrassment at never having attended college. Another client realized that his younger brother's voice was one of those that inhibited him from writing. "You know," he told me one day, "I'm just starting to understand that my younger brother always resented me for being in the family before he arrived. Not to mention that I was something of a jock. In fact, I remember him attributing what he called my lousy writing to my athletic ability. 'Give up. You're a football player—you can't write,' he used to say whenever he saw me working on a paper for English or history class."

When writers see the virulent animosity they direct at themselves, they realize what they are up against. Most important, they begin to acquire a degree of empathy for themselves. Some of them even rise up in their own defense.

"My sons and daughter like spending time with me," a mother of adult children told me, "so I can't be that bad!" "My awards in college, my promotions at work—that makes a lot of awfully well-educated people who have been mistaken about my ability," another writer mused. "This is so sad," a graduate student said, shaking her head in disbelief. "I feel terrible for myself." "I had no idea," a recent MBA said. "It's amazing I manage to get out of bed in the morning, I put myself under such a handicap."

As awful as I feel revealing to writers the degree of their self-directed abuse, I know it is an important step in getting them back on to their own side. Imagine trying to write with a chorus of detractors screaming derision at you and nobody standing by in support. Do you think André Agassi could win if all the fans at every match cheered only for his opponent and booed André? "Way to go, Michael. Beautiful shot. Terrific volley." "Boo, André! Lousy serve! You call yourself a tennis player? You're too sloppy to get this next shot. Clumsy oaf!" Not only would Agassi have difficulty winning; after a while he'd be lucky if his racket even connected with the ball!

It's helpful for us as blocked writers to recognize the face as well as the voice of our enemies. That way we know when it's wise to cross the street or take a different route home. We may even be able to devise strategies for negotiation or come up with responses to some of the criticism. "I might not be a great speller, but that doesn't mean I can't write. It simply means I can't *spell*." "If you think my weight has anything to do with my ability to write, *you're* the one who's mixed up." "You weren't the person in charge of my promotion. You might think I didn't deserve it, but my boss, who is intimately familiar with my writing, disagrees."

We might also realize that the critic's opinions are no longer relevant. "Mrs. Lauck, you were my fourth-grade teacher. And I appreciated you then. But I've already graduated from college.

Your comments are no longer called for." "Dad, I know you are disappointed in what I'm writing about. But I never wanted to be a doctor." "Mr. Di Filippi, just because I couldn't understand calculus in high school doesn't mean I can't write my novel!"

Some of the critics *may* be relevant to your writing, but have poorly timed their appearance. To those voices, like those of high-school English teachers or professors of composition and writing from college, I suggest offering a rain check, letting such critics know that their services will be of value later in the writing process, when the initial drafts are complete and copyediting for grammar, spelling, and punctuation is called for.

Flushing out your critics and devising strategies for diluting their power boosts you as a writer in several ways. Reducing the strength and number of naysayers places you that much closer to the act of writing itself. It is as if you have pushed aside several of the hurdles standing between your words and the blank page. What's more, understanding that you can dream up tactics for confronting, appeasing, banishing, even reasoning with your critics lessens feelings of vulnerability and helplessness. Instead of being blindsided each time you sit down to write, you can begin to shape the writing situation and experience, creating an environment in which you feel comfortable and safe to write.

People often ask me about the criticism I directed at myself during the years I suffered from writing block. They want to know that I struggled as acutely as they are struggling. They want to reassure themselves that if I recovered, they can too. The message I told myself, over and over, was that I could not write at all. It was that simple. I would read a sentence I'd composed and conclude that I hadn't found the best—the most comprehensive or cogent or concise or intelligent—way to articulate my idea. So I would rewrite and reread, each time deciding, *No, that's not it either.* And I would start in again, adding a preliminary or modifying clause to the sentence, or I'd try changing a few key words or inverting the syntax. Then, once I'd bent and twisted the initial sentence until it could no longer hold itself upright, I'd throw it away and start all over again, the whole time thinking, *I'm such a lousy writer.*

And yet this was not entirely accurate. It is true that I could not write in English. Yet when it came time to write for the classes I took toward my major, French literature, I became fluent on the page. I wrote with grace, about Andre Gide, Baudelaire, the French New Novel, Proust, Jacques Prévert, Corneille, Molière, Victor Hugo, Mallarmé, Alfred de Vigny, Ionesco, Albert Camus. In fact, my professors complimented me on my written French, and I graduated with high honors and an honors thesis on the French New Novel.

But I could not write in English. I told myself I could not. My professors told me I could not. And when, today, I read over some of the papers I turned in during those years of struggle, I can see for myself that I could not. I could not get my thoughts straight. Could not sort out what was essential and what was not. Could not begin and end sentences in a timely way; instead, I wrote by accumulation, the space between the first capitalization and the final period ponderous, ornate—and usually circuitous. Traveling from my head to the page, words and sentences were stunt airplanes, streaking by, circling, spinning, diving toward earth, then pulling out of the tailspin and heading back up into the heavens once again.

I can't write. This statement functions as a self-fulfilling prophecy. By repeating it over and over and over again, we make it come true. We not only come to believe in its veracity—in its literal, absolute truth—but through repetition, through coupling these words with each of our efforts to sit down and write, we can condition ourselves not to be able to write.

To undo a conditioned reponse takes time. Unfortunately, one traumatic event can create a strong association. One cruel word, one misstep, one moment of hesitation in front of an audience, and we never again want to speak in public or climb a ladder or sit down to write. It takes much, much longer to undo the damage. I once backed up into another car in a downtown parking structure. Luckily, I was moving very slowly, so I left no mark. Still, for months afterward, no matter how many times I peered into my rearview mirror, I felt shaky each time I began to pull out of my parking space in a garage. Associations like this can lead us to avoid routine activities out of fear that the unpleasant experience will be repeated.

The first phase in the uncoupling process involves separating the two activities we have been bringing into intimate contact. For blocked writers this means eliminating self-accusation from the writing process. At first we all need reminders. That's why I often stop clients mid-sentence when I sense self-criticism looming. Taking them by surprise this way may create a strong enough impression that they can catch themselves on their own in the future. Other writers need more coaching—as well as coaxing—and in these cases I work particularly hard on flushing out the writers' critics and devising strategies to disarm the chorus of voices that has become louder and louder over the years. Eventually, even those writers most intent on directing anger at themselves catch on. They recognize for the first time the gauntlet they have to run in order to write, and they understand why they began to avoid writing in the first place. For them, to write is to expose themselves to self-punishment, each word a weapon that will be used against them. Understanding this danger, they can begin to see that it's not because they write best to deadline, or because they are disorganized, that they cannot sit down to write. It is because writing inevitably exposes them to a barrage of their own insults and criticism. Knowing, even unconsciously, that we are setting ourselves up as targets for such intense abuse, we understandably avoid writing in any way possible. We schedule ourselves until we are dizzy, or we wait until the very last minute. No wonder the blank page can seem so threatening. Filling it may cause us harm. Realizing this, understanding that it is because we are afraid—and of what—comes as a relief. "Phew," one writer said recently. "So it's not because I'm lazy." Another client, who had spent thousands of dollars on organization consultants, told me that believing that chaos—on her desk and in her office and life—was the root of her problem made her believe the space in her head was chaotic as well. Just knowing that her writing problem wasn't the result of disorganization allowed her to think clearly once again.

Last night, at a meeting of an advanced workshop, one of the writers, a seasoned journalist who had recently experienced what she now refers to as a "writer's nervous breakdown," started to preface her work with her habitual self-criticism. "I hate what I'm about to read to you. . . ." she began. Then she caught herself. I watched as she took a deep breath, color returning to her face, straightened her elegant, slender frame in the chair, made eye contact with the other writers in the circle, and continued. "No, I'm not going to say that. Instead, I'm going to tell you that I'm proud of myself for being here tonight." As she read her two-page proposal for the project she hopes to complete this year, her voice gained strength and confidence. By the end of the evening, she communicated an acumen and authority that until then had always hovered just below the surface of her presence.

This woman had been a professional writer for over a decade when, suddenly, sitting down to begin an assignment caused her so much anxiety she had to stop writing for several years. Last night she was able to catch herself mid-abuse because she had already laid the groundwork for improving her relationship with writing. We had worked together after her two-year silence to devise strategies to help her return to writing without stirring up the storm clouds she feared would gather. And despite the fact that she was thoroughly cooperative, it took several months for the self-criticism to stop.

Working to step away from the role of our own harshest critics is pivotal to overcoming writing blocks. The role is one we learn from those around us; we take to heart our lines, initially provided by those in authority, and eventually we perform as if they were our own. We are so gullible as children, so absorbent, that we take in whatever our parents and our teachers tell us about ourselves. When I was in the fourth grade, my teacher terrorized most of the children in her class. Her black hair pulled back in a tight bun, her back rigid, E. Dora Lauck held us to the highest standards. In the middle of the year, we moved into a new building, and the entire school was to participate in the laying of the cornerstone. Part of the ceremony involved collecting sheets with the signatures of the students in every classroom. Mrs. Lauck gave us instructions on how and where to sign the thick white sheet, then began walking up and down the rows as the paper was passed from student to student. I sat in the third seat in the first row on the left side of the room. As soon as I closed the last loop in my surname, Pomerantz, Mrs. Lauck snatched the sheet from my desk and held it up for all to ridicule. "I told you to sign your name in a straight line. See how Jane Anne's runs downhill. This will not do. We're going to have to start all over again, all because Jane Anne couldn't follow instructions." All these many years later I still feel a twinge of panic whenever I'm asked to fill out a form and sign my name.

Mrs. Lauck was my first critic. I had others along the way, their lines so much easier to memorize than to forget. The same holds for any writer who experiences difficulty with writing, no matter how extensive and prolonged. Jettisoning these voices, one by one, day by day, requires vigilance. But imagine how much lighter and safer we feel once we have shed them.

Try This

1. Set aside fifteen minutes to write. As you write, tune into the voices in your head and keep a record of what they say. You can do this by quoting these voices within the body of your text, by opening a second computer file, or by keeping a notebook or extra sheet of paper by your side. Do this several times within a week, and don't be surprised if the voices increase in intensity or quantity.

2. Once you have recorded these voices, try to identify each one, along with the role he or she played in your life. If you have difficulty identifying any of them, read aloud what they have to say, then close your eyes, letting their words float in the air around you. Does this help you recognize the speakers?

3. Ask yourself questions like: "Is the voice of my sixth-grade teacher relevant to me today?" "Why was my father so critical of my writing when I was in high school? Was his criticism directed at me, or is it possible that he was criticizing himself at the same time?" "Why should my sister care what kind of writer I am?"

4. If you have been able to identify your enemies, you may begin responding to their criticisms. You might say something like, "Mr. Diver, I really don't think I need your help anymore. You taught me a lot about history when I was eleven years old. But my dissertation has nothing to do with history or with me as an elementary school student." Or, "Dad, I'm sorry you never wrote the novel you've been

thinking about writing all your life. I know you must feel disappointed, but that is no reason to inhibit my ability to write." Or, if the critic is not completely irrelevant to your writing project, you might say, "Professor Gilbert, you really helped me with my expository writing in college. And I'm sure I could still use your help. But not right now. Let me finish a draft or two, and then I'll call on you. I promise."

4

First Words

During the first weeks of every new workshop, when I ask students if anything noteworthy happened during their writing week, someone always remarks about how difficult it was to get started. Heads begin to nod, and quickly the classroom is abuzz. "It was almost impossible." "You said it. I was like a jack-in-the-box, popping up and down for the longest time." "I must have cleaned every surface in my kitchen before I could even walk past my computer." "I didn't begin until last night." Just when I begin to wonder if anyone in the class wrote anything at all, a student always pipes up, "But you know what? Once I got myself to sit down and begin typing, I discovered that it wasn't so bad after all." Again heads nod, this time even more forcefully. "That's exactly what happened to me," another writer concurs. "As a matter of fact, after I'd written a first draft, I realized that I'd kind of enjoyed myself once I got started." Again, all around the room heads are bobbing, and I utter a silent *Phew!*

As we continue our discussion, I discover that at least one-third of the workshop has had this breakthrough experience: once they placed themselves in front of their computer or poised their pen above the blank page, they were indeed able to write. Their difficulty was not in gathering words and placing them within a text. Contrary to what they feared, they did not have a writing problem after all; what they had was a problem *sitting down*. For them the mere thought of writing was so intimidating that they avoided even the first step to putting words on the page: Instead of pulling up a chair and settling in, they kept moving. Once they were able to remain in place, they could send down roots, their writing sprouted stems and leaves, and it gradually bore fruit.

It's wonderful when blocked writers discover on their own that, if they can simply sit down—on a chair, the banks of a creek, a bench in the park—and begin putting words on the page, writing no longer looms so formidable. What once held the power of a *Tyrannosaurus rex* shrinks to the size of an iguana. And if in the following weeks they can recall the relief of finally sitting down and allowing words to find their way onto the page, they will experience much less discomfort at the prospect of writing. They will think of the week's writing project, experience a flicker of anxiety, and then calm themselves immediately by remembering that, once they sit down and initiate the act of writing, their discomfort will begin to subside. Understanding that their resistance is to something as ordinary as sitting down, these writers are finally able, quite literally, to put themselves in a position to write.

But there are other writers, plenty of them, who cannot make this discovery on their own. For these writers even sitting down with pen in hand feels devastating. One step closer to the seat, and they risk their lives. Of course, this is not what these writers tell themselves when they think about writing. The words themselves, the consciousness of their fear, have been buried so deep within their psyches that they are not aware of their motives. All they are aware of is *not writing*. Some do not even realize that they are anxious. Instead, their lives feel too complex and busy to allow them time for writing. They have too many family obligations, or too heavy a work schedule, or too many guests, or too much work

to do in the garden. After my own years of block, as well as working with so many writers who have been unable to complete
their dissertations, write their tenure review articles, finish the
novel their publisher has been expecting for the past three
months, I know how easy it is, when we are anxious or worried
about writing, to fill our lives with enough busyness that we can
easily believe there simply isn't any time left to write. This hyper-
activity is a creative way of boycotting writing. Though we are
not signing petitions or marching in protest, we are boycotting
just the same. Ours is a type of passive resistance. By not finding
the time or the energy to write, we are making an implicit statement: everything else in my life is more important than my
writing!

For some writers the prospect of writing can provoke an anxiety so severe that they boycott not only their computer but the
room where they keep it. One of my clients, a doctoral student,
had set up her desk and study area in her bedroom, and by the
time she came to see me, she had begun sleeping on the sofa. "I
can't sleep with the computer in the same room; I have nightmares," she confessed. Another writer was avoiding her living
room for the same reason. The computer was located there, and
each time it came into her line of sight, a shot of adrenaline
coursed through her. "I no longer have a social life," she revealed.
"After all, you can't invite people directly into your bedroom!"

For these writers the first step in overcoming their block is to
make writing feel safe. To do this we need to reduce the valence
of writing, to diminish its negative charge. To put writing in its
place. Because they are so worried about not writing, feel so
guilty about not doing their work, so disappointed about not
realizing their dreams, writing looms larger and larger, until they
think about what they are *not* doing constantly, obsessively, and

the words they are unable to put on the page seep into every nook and cranny of their lives. After a while some of these writers can no longer enjoy themselves, so preoccupied have they become with what they feel they *should* be doing. One of my clients told me she hadn't even been to a movie in the past year. "Whenever I think about going out, I immediately point a finger at myself. 'You can't have fun. You need to stay home and write.'" Another client realized that if she had only written for one-fourth of the time she thought about writing, already she could have written her dissertation plus the book she would need to be granted tenure.

To put writing in its place, you have to shrink it down to dimensions that allow you to fit it into your life. One simple way to do this is to give yourself permission to write for fifteen minutes each day. If fifteen minutes raises goose bumps, try ten or even five minutes. What matters is not how long you write, but simply the fact of writing. If you haven't been able to write a word, you'll be thrilled to have written anything at all. The goal right now is to shift your response to writing from negative to positive. Limiting your writing time to a brief interlude lowers the threat-quotient. The prospect of feeling anxious for four hours at a stretch is unbearable, but most of us are willing to risk fifteen minutes of discomfort. And once we experience the pleasure of survival, we can begin to accumulate good feelings about writing.

Unfortunately, most blocked writers do just the opposite. They become increasingly punitive toward themselves, and after some time their negative attitudes expand far beyond the act of writing itself. They decide they are lazy and escapist. Unmotivated. Disorganized. Confused. That, if they are going to get anywhere in life, they must finally toe the line. So they sentence themselves to write, setting aside a week, crossing everything else off their calendars and planning to write for at least eight hours a day. Or to write a chapter a day. Or their entire dissertation proposal in one week. "Is it any surprise that you began avoiding writing even more after that?" I ask clients who have shackled themselves in this way. "If I thought that all I was allowed to do for an entire week was to write, I would become blocked, too."

More serious is the issue of punishment. Unable to write, feeling more and more frustrated and less and less competent, these writers punish themselves. "No fun for you until you've finished your dissertation." "No music until that memo is distributed." "No walks until you write every single word of that brief." Not only do they deny themselves all pleasure, they take out their emotional whips and begin lashing. "You don't deserve to have any fun. You've had too much fun already; that's why you haven't finished your tenure article." "You love to drink fine wine, but you don't deserve one drop until you complete that grant proposal."

Writers don't have to be blocked for long before they engage in psychological capital punishment. Just this week in my University of California Berkeley Extension workshop, a spunky young woman in her mid-twenties, a graduate of an Ivy League college, raised her hand and announced, "I don't know what my problem is. I just can't seem to sit down and write. I need somebody to tell me I'm grounded next weekend." As I listened, sirens began to go off in my head. I knew that within weeks this energetic, fun-loving twenty-five-year-old would strip her life of pleasure if she didn't begin to write.

The best way to reverse this type of rut is to realize that most of us have the wrong idea about motivation. How can we expect that being so severe with ourselves will motivate us to do something we have been avoiding? Being negative only makes matters worse. If writing already provokes discomfort, self-inflicted punishment creates anguish. Negative reinforcement is part of the Dark Ages of psychology. We no longer even train dogs by using punishment. In Berkeley, most families with puppies attend training classes where rewards—not punishments or corrections—are the order of the day. Each time your puppy performs the desired behavior, you offer it a treat. You say, "Sit," and if the puppy drops to its haunches, you offer it a piece of jerky. If the puppy fails to sit, you lure it into a sitting position and then reward him. In no time your dog feels safe with you and happily obeys your commands, his tongue hanging in anticipation of a treat.

To write you must feel safe. Punishment and harshness threaten us, put us at risk. Why would sensible people, knowing that they will be punished if they fail, want to pull up a chair and begin to write? Why would any of us purposefully or deliberately expose ourselves to deprivation? Wouldn't it make more sense to take the opposite approach? To think about the ways we can *entice* ourselves to write—the rewards we can offer ourselves for doing something we do not look forward to doing?

A more sophisticated explanation than common sense involves conditioning. If writers who already feel uncomfortable about writing try to motivate themselves to write with threats and punishments, they strengthen their negative associations with writing, and by strengthening these negative associations they avoid writing all the more. Most of us have learned about classical conditioning, which can quickly train animals to avoid any behavior associated with even a small electrical shock, and, conversely, to enact any behavior followed by an offering of food. It makes sense, then, that instead of emotionally shocking ourselves our goal should be to condition ourselves *positively* toward putting words on the page.

This method, also referred to as behavior modification, has been used effectively in schools for autistic children, where the teachers offer M&Ms to reward good behavior. Each time a student looks the teacher in the eye, for example, or speaks or stops running in circles, the teacher gives that student an M&M. After enough repetition, the brightly colored candies condition the autistic students to enact the desired behavior on their own.

The blocked writer's equivalent to M&Ms is kindness. Getting those first words onto the page deserves it. Instead of giving themselves M&Ms, blocked writers must learn to whisper sweet nothings into their own ears. These words will be different for each one of us. An expression as simple as, "You've done it!" may work, especially at the beginning, before we've tuned in more intimately to our vulnerabilities. Other writers find that simply countering the punitive messages they'd been telegramming to themselves is helpful. "See, you're not lazy." Or, "You haven't wasted the whole day; you've gotten something done!" Or, "You've met your goal." Or, "You did what you planned to do." Of course, "You're off to a good start" is always uplifting for writers who for years have been unable to begin. What counts is not the words themselves, but the message behind them. Kindness, celebration, compassion, approval—any of these reinforces the simple act of sitting down to write, the first step in overcoming writing block.

After a period of time—different for each of us—some blocked writers discover that, without being conscious of changing their message, they have begun whispering new, even-sweeter nothings to themselves. One writer whose block was intermittent—she would write for several months, then find herself unable to sit down for several more—discovered herself repeating, "You've been writing for three months now, Jeannie. That's wonderful!" A psychologist I worked with realized that baseball metaphors had begun flashing into his thoughts. "Hey, man, you've just hit a double," he'd hear a voice telling him. Or, "This one might be a homer." This client had once been a baseball star, beginning with little league and continuing into college. After he began to feel better about sitting down to write, he found himself returning to his childhood passion.

Another reward for getting those first words onto the page is the promise of pleasure. If all you have to do is write for fifteen minutes before you can go for a walk, listen to your favorite CD, read a chapter of a fine novel, call a friend, romp with your pup, the thought of writing will not be so unpleasant. Some of your anticipated pleasure will seep in through the cracks of your anxiety, making it just a bit easier to sit down. And then when you cap your pen or log off your computer, the relief of having met your goal and the joy or satisfaction of your next activity will commingle, casting a new and more golden light upon writing.

I often suggest to clients who continue to find it difficult to sit down and begin writing that they make an appointment to leave their house or apartment immediately following their writing time. A haircut, car inspection, medical checkup, facial—it doesn't really matter. Simply knowing that you really *must* stop at the appointed time makes sitting down all that much easier. Don't worry that you will feel guilty getting up after only a quarter of an hour. You have another obligation that needs your attention. One of my clients, who had slowly worked her way up to writing for one hour a day, made a date to go walking with a friend every weekday at noon. This client had experienced the advantage of limiting her writing time, and she didn't want to become tempted to extend it prematurely. As long as she knew her friend would be waiting for her in front of her apartment, she was in no danger of overexposing herself. In addition, the walk was a reward for the writing she had done.

Rewards at the end of the writing period have a circular effect on the writing process. Not only do they transform the completion of the act of writing into a positive experience, they recast the initiation as well. Because we anticipate subsequent pleasure, it is that much easier to sit down and begin writing. Having something to look forward to creates a rainbow that arches over our writing from beginning to end.

Acknowledging the isolation that accompanies writing may help alleviate some of our anxiety. Putting words on the page is a solitary act; when we write, we are alone. "This is ridiculous," a friend announced one day. "I have no trouble going out to my garden each morning. Why is it so much harder to write? It doesn't make any sense." But I understood. The thought of a solo hike is not half as enticing as anticipating climbing up into the hills with a companion. While writing is a solo act, my friend was not alone in her garden. Gardening is a collaboration. She had plants as company and inspiration, surrounding her with color, texture, and scent. Sitting down to write, she faced a blank page. No nursery or orchard could supply the words; no landscape artist could help her place them on the page. Everything depended on her. "I might as well be a magician pulling rabbits out of a hat when I write," she said—that's how mysterious the process of writing felt to her. "But I can make anything grow."

"Why don't you try writing in your garden?" I suggested. "Perhaps that way your plants will keep you company and encourage the magic."

Writing in a place you enjoy can be like soaking up the sun before you dive into the cold waters of a mountain lake. Or meeting a close friend at the trailhead for your hike. The comfort of place can make you feel less alone and help tease those first words onto the page. The scene of my first full unblocking was a diner just outside Iowa City. I was interning with a professor of writing that semester and had decided to complete the assignments along with the class. I thought that observing a gifted professor teach freshmen to write might help me overcome my own difficulties. One of the first assignments was to describe a scene, any scene, and I had already made several false starts. The day before the assignment was due, I left my house, writing materials in hand, to get a cup of coffee. Maybe that would help me write, I thought. As I sat in a booth of that local diner, I tried to recall the scene I had originally intended to capture on the page: the bus stop across the street from our house. I could see the stop clearly from my study and thought it was a good candidate for the assignment. But I had not been able to get more than a sentence or two onto the page before crumpling up the paper and tossing it into the wastebasket.

Sitting in the diner, the click and clatter of cups and saucers and the low buzz of talk all around me, I tried to recall what the stop had looked like the last time I sat and observed it—the weather, the people waiting, the cars passing. The waitress came by my table to refill my coffee cup, and when she left, I followed her with my eyes as she moved from booth to booth, pouring coffee, taking orders, chatting with customers. Almost without knowing it I began writing about what I saw. I described the waitress's auburn hair and the braid down her back. Her wasp-thin waist. Her white shoes. I turned the page, transcribing the conversation between the two farmers at the next booth. They were discussing the price of hogs. By the time my second coffee cup was empty, I had filled four pages with description.

At first I thought it was the subject matter that had allowed me to write such fluent prose. But then I realized that a more important difference between my experience that day in the diner and my usual struggle to write was *place*. My desk at home was associated with hours of hand-wringing attempts to write, with wad after wad of paper I had failed to fill, with hours of disappointment and self-doubt. The diner, on the other hand, held a more positive valence. I associated being there with relaxing and socializing with friends, with the back-and-forth of conversations or the flights of daydreaming. The diner did not arouse my usual writing panic. No digging in my heels and stiffening my knees against malaise or discomfort, no heart-thumping flights to safety. Ensconced in the booth, surrounded by the white noise of the café, I was safe, my words free to find their way outside my head and into the light.

You don't always need dramatic shifts in place to help you write. Sometimes it's as simple as setting a vase of fresh flowers on your desk. The scent of roses or the colors of a spring bouquet invite you to sit down and inhale or gaze, and before you know it, you have begun to write. Filling the walls surrounding your desk with photographs or artwork can draw you out of your habitual writing discomfort into a place of warmth and ease. Pictures of friends and family can create a gallery of support for blocked writers. Scenes from trips you have taken may open the writing space to a time you felt expansive and full of possibility. A backdrop of your favorite music can inspire you. One of my clients discovered that she writes best while listening to Celtic music. When she went to Europe last summer, she made a tape of favorite tracks from her most prized CDs to take with her. Listening to her tapes when she was away from home helped ease the transition from not writing to typing those first words onto her laptop screen. Now she plays music while writing at home, too.

Framing time with positive experiences also helps change our associations with writing. Instead of working on her dissertation, one of my clients found herself practicing the part she was to sing in the concert her choir was going to perform. "Instead of denying yourself all pleasure in order to write, why don't you indulge yourself for a while with singing?" I suggested. "Rehearse your part in the oratorio for fifteen minutes or so each morning, then sit down to write. And when you are finished writing, sing some more." Many people find that a period of meditation before sitting down to write helps them accomplish the most difficult of transitions: pulling up a chair and starting to write.

Another client once mentioned that she had a lifelong passion for beads. Indeed, even though she wasn't in the habit of using the beads, she had a vast collection of them in her study, all organized by color and size. Together we realized that creating key chains with these beautiful beads would give her a great deal of pleasure, and that she could sandwich her writing sessions between sessions of beading. This worked so well that she eventually began using the key chains as a focus for her writing, describing the beads themselves, the process of stringing them, and the people to whom she offered the chains once they were completed.

The atmosphere we create for ourselves is an essential factor in our relationship with writing. Poor acoustics, a weed-choked pond, a dim studio—each interferes with the activity it is intended to promote. We cannot become lost in a violin concerto if the sound reaching us is fuzzy, glide through cool water if our fingers become entangled in weeds, or begin painting if we have to strain to see our model's face. In the same way, discomfort and anxiety around writing make it impossible to capture those first words on the page. Providing the right space, multiplying positive associations, and rewarding ourselves for actually sitting down and connecting to the page are all means for creating an atmosphere that eases the transition from not writing to writing. The particular ingredients we combine to create this atmosphere will be different for each of us.

During the first weeks of my workshops through U.C. Berkeley Extension, I ask my students to observe themselves as writers over the semester, noticing what in their individual writing situations and approaches feels comfortable to them, what seems to help them write, and what gets in their way. "And once you know all the ingredients that help you sit down and begin, be certain that you don't omit any in the future," I urge. This is one of the benefits of becoming a writer. You have permission to indulge yourself. Perhaps for the first time you can tell your children or your boyfriend, "Look, I need to write, and your music interferes. Could you please turn it off for the next hour?" You can buy yourself flowers. Take a trip to the record store. Rearrange your apartment. Go out to your favorite restaurant or café for lunch.

To write you have to take writing seriously. And to take writing seriously, you have to take *yourself* seriously. This means being exquisitely sensitive to yourself. To what supports and nurtures your writing. To whatever helps you begin and allows those first words to find their way into your text. Now, for perhaps the only time in your life, you have permission to think of yourself first. So be selfish! Do whatever you can think of to lure the initial words onto the page. From then on you just might be swimming with the current.

Try This

1. Plan to reward yourself after your writing session. A bike ride, a lunch date, a walk around the block, listening to your favorite CD—any activity you look forward to can help you overcome your resistance to sitting down to write.

2. Try sitting quietly for several minutes, listening to music perhaps, or breathing deeply, and invite yourself to begin writing. Say to yourself, "You are going to begin writing in a few minutes. And there's nothing to be afraid of. You're going to write for fifteen minutes only, and after that you're free to go for a walk. Just relax, and don't worry. I'll be there with you."

3. If sitting down to write feels difficult, create a definitive stopping point. For a month or two schedule all your household appointments at the same time every day. Make an appointment to change the oil in your car, to see your doctor, to get a haircut, to talk to your accountant. Sign up for a month-long yoga or exercise class. Make a date to walk your dog with a friend every day at the same time. Or create a writing buddy to check in with on schedule when you finish each session.

4. If you engage on a regular basis in any activity that gives you pleasure and a sense of confidence, it can help to visualize yourself engaged in this activity before you begin writing. If you swim, for example, you might close your eyes and imagine yourself swimming, stroking and kicking effortlessly as you glide from one end of the pool to the other, and back again.

5. Once you have been writing regularly for a week or two, tune in once again to the voices in your head. Have they diminished? Do you notice any new members of the chorus? Any voices that sound approving? That give you compliments like, *You did it!*, or, *See how organized and disciplined you've become.*

5

Thinking Small

If I were to choose a mantra for my writing, it would be *Think small*. Each time I sit down to write, I begin by recalling these two words. And whenever I feel myself slowing down too much or veering offtrack, I bring myself back by repeating them. *Think small, Jane Anne. Think small.*

When I talk to my workshops about thinking small, which I do always within the first two weeks, I can expect several of the writers sitting in front of me to look disgusted—to say nothing of all those whose disappointment seeps into their eyes. They have registered for this course and paid good money for it, and they are burning to write. One has been practicing Zen meditation for the past ten years and has made important discoveries he wants to communicate. Another has insights won during a painful divorce and knows they will help other women struggling with the same situation. A third is bursting with stories from her yearlong trek through Asia. How dare I urge them to think small!

Before they can raise their hands and begin arguing with me, I tell these eager writers not to worry, to hear me out. "Think Small" is one of the paradoxes I have discovered about writing. Thinking small actually helps us write big. Instead of limiting you, thinking small will set you free. Will make it possible to tell your truths, reveal your insights, and tell your stories. Believe it or not, trouble starts when we think too big. When we give ourselves too much room to wander, to become distracted, to feel overwhelmed.

Think too big, and you'll find yourself at the base of Anapurna, aiming for the summit, when you've not yet attempted Half Dome. Sure, you've worked out for the past year, read everything you could get your hands on about mountaineering, joined a group of climbers led by a famous guide. And you're determined. So, gazing skyward, you set off. But within the first five hundred yards, you fall behind. Already you feel discouraged and wonder if you should turn back. But you push on. *Nobody said this would be easy,* you think to yourself. *Just put one foot in front of the other.* Soon you fall behind again, but this time, struggling to keep the pace, you twist an ankle. *You're never going to make it,* you hear a voice scolding from somewhere deep in your head. *Give up now. Turn back.*

"Does any of this sound familiar?" I ask, and heads begin to nod. "That's me," someone always calls out. "Me too!" another student echoes. Heads bob throughout the room. It feels as if someone has just turned down the volume. It is early in the semester, and most of the workshop still arrives full of the tension and uncertainty a writing class can provoke. *Will I be able to write? Will I accomplish all I want? Will my work be well received?* "Think small," I say, and once they have begun to understand the message, it comes as a relief.

Thinking big is what got me in trouble. And still trips me up if I forget to catch myself—which doesn't happen often now that I've learned to watch for telltale signs: a rapid pulse, a queasy feeling in my gut, drumming in my head, dryness in my mouth, stiff neck. At any of these signs I pause and take a reading. Usually I see that my net, sized to catch the small stuff—anchovies, sardines, and haddock—has swelled. I have tossed it farther and farther out, trying to catch ever-bigger fish, and now my sights are set on whales.

My habit of thinking big began in college. The chain of events used to look like this: I might be assigned a paper on *Hamlet* for my Shakespeare class on a Monday during the first month of the semester. Before I left the classroom that day, I would leap ahead to finals week and the Shakespeare term paper I would also have to write. After all, my grade depended on my work for the entire semester, so why worry only about the assignment due within a month? And while I was concerned with Shakespeare, what was I going to write for my Hinduism take-home midterm? And what about sociology? And I should never have signed up for a course on Wittgenstein. I would never really understand his *Philosophical Investigations*. My grades were going to slip. My grade-point average would be ruined. No decent graduate school would want me. I would never find a teaching position once I'd finished. I might even remain unemployed. A Ph.D. without a future. A failure!

This is the first strategy for thinking big. This is snowballing. Never staying in the moment, never looking at what's right in front of you. Instead, you jump ahead to tomorrow, to next week, next month, next year. It means not focusing on what you have to do today, right now. Instead, you roll your fist-sized ball of snow all the way to the base of the mountain until it has grown so huge it blocks your path.

After the first night of my U.C. Berkeley Extension class last semester, a student asked me if I thought he should drop the course. "I might have to miss two or three classes because of work. I don't know yet, but I usually have to travel at least once a month. And I may have houseguests for a weekend or two, and that would make it difficult for me to write. Also, I have some family business I ought to look after. Do you think I should bother coming next week?"

This too is snowballing. The student, an accountant with a large firm, did indeed travel to see clients out of town. But only for a day or two, and he could usually rearrange his schedule. The houseguests were not confirmed; they had only mentioned that they might be coming to San Francisco within the next month or so. And the family business was ongoing and could easily be postponed. But because this student was worried about the workshop, about whether he had writing talent or not, he thought big. He thought about every possible distraction and obligation that would take him away from writing, until he felt completely overwhelmed—and was convinced that he shouldn't take the class.

Accumulating obstacles to writing is snowballing. A graduate student I worked with several years ago snowballed in an even-larger way. She came to see me because she had been unable to begin her dissertation. She knew her topic and was interested in the material, but she had been trying to write her proposal for months and had nothing to show for her effort. She told me that, whenever she decided to write, she immediately thought about looking for a job once she had her Ph.D. "Then I decide that, before I sit down, I should see if any new positions at a college or university anywhere in the San Francisco area have been posted. So I log onto the Web or run up to campus to check."

This client's dissertation proposal was her fist-sized snowball. Once she set it rolling, it picked up layer after layer of snow and debris: *If I write my proposal, I will have to begin my dissertation. If I begin my dissertation, I may finish it and receive my degree. If I receive my degree, I will have to look for a job. But the job market is restricted now. I won't have much to choose from, and I'll probably have to move away. But my husband may not want to leave. His family lives here. His job is here. And he may not be able to find another he's qualified for. He hates to interview. I'd better try to find work here. But this is a competitive area, and I have never taught. I need teaching experience if I want a job. . . .*

Snowballing is one way of distracting ourselves from writing. Whether or not we are aware of our discomfort at the prospect of putting words onto the page, creating a list of all our obligations—actual and potential, real and imaginary—is a strategy to keep our anxiety at bay. "I can't write until I figure out my schedule for the rest of the semester," I used to tell myself in college. *I can't write until I find a teaching position,* my graduate student thought. Of course, at first we aren't aware of the barrage of messages we keep telegramming to ourselves. All we know is that, every time we sit down to write, we think of everything else we should be doing. It is not until we understand our snowballing that we grasp the length of the "to do" list we have been reciting to ourselves.

At first making schedules, creating agendas, ticking off lists, and anticipating future term-paper topics all help to keep us calm. No need to feel guilty about not beginning a dissertation proposal, a letter to an old friend, or the office memo for this week— we have to organize our lives first. But snowballing backfires. Instead of remaining calm, we shift to feeling overwhelmed as the snowball swells into an avalanche that threatens to engulf us.

One of my clients, a well-known economist, came to me because he was having difficulty writing a book he had been thinking about for the past ten years. "I want to explain macroeconomic theory in an intelligent and available way, so that any well-educated reader will be able to follow my logic," he told me when we first met. His goal sounded reasonable, and he seemed levelheaded, so I was optimistic about helping him move on. We spent a session or two discussing his first chapter, and he set to work. *This is exciting,* I thought. *He's writing an important book, and he's going to make it.* I decided that all he lacked was an attentive audience for what he wanted to say, and now that he was working with me, he had that audience. Then, just when he was about to finish the first chapter and move on to the second, my client decided to rewrite what he had written. "I'm not sure I like the tone," he told me. "I want to see if I can sound more relaxed on the page." Next he decided he had diluted his material too much, and he rewrote the chapter to incorporate footnotes and references into the text. After that, it was the structure he found fault with. "I don't think I'm presenting the material in the best possible order," he told me, explaining this latest revision.

I said we needed to talk. And when I penetrated the thinking behind his successive revisions, I realized my client wanted his book to be the *World Book* and *Encyclopedia Britannica* of economics rolled into one. He wanted to explain all of macroeconomic theory so that the average reader could understand, and at the same time he hoped professional economists and scholars would appreciate his fine mind. This is what I call telescoping, taking too wide or long a view of a writing project and trying to cover all the material we see through the lens in one term paper, one essay, or one book.

Telescoping is a form of ambition, of thinking too big about how much we want to write, the material we want to cover, the audience we want to reach. It is trying to include too much information, embracing too large a topic, focusing on too many readers. It is trying to write a twelve-page term paper on the theme of greed in *all* of Shakespeare's tragedies. It is deciding to describe the entire garden instead of one flower. Arguing for the concept of individual freedom instead of for free speech.

When I taught in the freshman English department at Stanford University, around midterm students began coming to my office asking for help with papers for other courses. "I don't know where to start," they would tell me. Or, "I'll never have time to do all the research." And, "I've begun this paper three times, but I keep heading in the wrong direction." When I'd ask these students what they were writing about, they would name topics so vast, I could feel myself sinking. "Think small" was the life vest I tossed to each of them. And together we would rethink the topic, narrowing its focus until they were left with something manageable, specific, and . . . *small.*

If our appetite is too grand, and the vistas we imagine are too vast, we need to move closer to what we want to write or write about. We must remember to zoom in instead of panning out, to leave the grand scenes, the definitive tomes for later. In college I needed blinders to limit myself to the assignment at hand, to block out final exams and papers, grade-point averages and graduate degrees, to keep me on track in the present, away from time warps and future travel. Once my graduate student began reminding herself to stick to her proposal and to stop thinking about teaching and relocating and her husband's future, she was able to begin to write and was soon admitted to candidacy. Since he couldn't please all readers at the same time, the economist decided to aim his book at educated laymen and *later* to write a professional article. Getting into the new habit of thinking small was a challenge. He needed frequent reminders, and on occasion he would lapse, announcing that he had found a way "to do it all." Eventually, with lots of practice, he was able to laugh at his lapses, admitting that he still longed to think big but knew the only way to succeed was by thinking small.

When I took my four-month-old puppy to her first obedience class, the trainer divided the hour-long session into alternating segments of work and play. We would spend ten minutes teaching our pups to sit, then dismiss them to romp about the park. When we returned to our training, we began a new lesson, teaching them to stay or to lie down, coming back to "sit" later, after another play break. At the end of the hour, the trainer reminded us to keep our work sessions short. "They're pups. They get tired and bored quickly. You don't want to turn them off."

Blocked writers need to treat themselves like pups. Too often they set grand goals for themselves. If they haven't gotten any writing done in a while, they may clear the decks completely, canceling all appointments and dates for the entire week, planning to be at their computer first thing Monday morning and to sit there every day, all week long, so they can finally get something accomplished. It is often after a few of these marathon streaks—after trying to take control, to stop procrastinating and start producing, with nothing to show for their effort—that they realize they need help.

Once you understand that thinking big is only going to get you into hot water, you can create a writing schedule. Sometimes it is best to write for only fifteen minutes each day for several weeks and renegotiate after that. If the block is recent or not deeply entrenched, you might manage to begin with a half hour—at the most one hour—per day. Limiting writing time is a way of conditioning yourself to think small. Short sessions will put the brakes on the merry-go-round of recrimination. If you're *allowed* to write for *only* fifteen minutes a day, then you're less likely to feel guilty about not writing more. Even better, you will quickly find that instead of feeling bad you'll begin to feel good. At the end of your allotted writing time, you might even find yourself patting yourself on the back: "There, I've done what I promised to do." Like money in the bank, these positive feelings accumulate. One day they will tip the scale and make it easier for you to sit down and write.

Thinking small, timewise, is the best insurance against avalanches. With short sessions we don't have the time or inclination to gather too much around us, focusing on an ever-growing list of associations with what we are trying to write. Short sessions keep us on track. The more we wander, the more we lose ourselves among the sand dunes and vastness of the desert. But how many wrong turns can a hiker make in fifteen quick minutes?

Last year a professor of psychology came to see me. Since being granted tenure fifteen years earlier, he had not been able to complete a single article for publication. Before his tenure review he had accumulated an impressive bibliography of publications, including many considered groundbreaking in his field. But since then, although he had begun many articles, he had abandoned each and every one midstream. "When I start writing an article, I usually feel pretty good and optimistic, but I quickly become discouraged. I tell myself that what I am writing just isn't all that important. Or that somebody else could do it better. And once that thought enters my head, no matter how hard I try, I can't work on that particular topic any longer. After a few months or maybe a year, I'll get excited about a different topic. 'This one really matters,' I'll tell myself. 'My colleagues will consider it a real contribution to the field. It's right up my alley.' And I start writing, full of enthusiasm. Pretty quickly, however, I become discouraged. And within a week or two I'm convinced that what I'm writing about is trivial, a waste of time."

I explained to this writer the importance of thinking small, and as I talked, he nooded enthusiastically. "Yes, that's my problem precisely! I can't think small enough. Whenever I begin to write, I get ahead of myself and start worrying about the impact my article will have on the entire field. That's what defeats me every single time."

Together the professor and I devised a plan to help contain his ambition and limit his horizon. First we decided that he would begin by writing for only thirty minutes each day—not one minute more. Then we discussed all the articles he had abandoned in the past ten years, with the goal of selecting the topic that was the most modest in scope, the one that would best allow him to limit the ambition that landed on his shoulders each time he began to write. I also suggested he write the rules for the project on an index card he could keep in front of him as he worked. On the card he noted that he would write for only thirty minutes a day. That his goal was to complete one publishable article—not more. And that in the article he did not expect to make a major contribution to his discipline. Instead, he hoped only to correct what he considered an erroneous interpretation of a well-known behavior. *Period!*

For the first few months I noticed that he kept trying to push the envelope, broadening the scope of his conclusions, bringing in arguments from other disciplines. Each time, I reminded him gently to review his goals for the piece. Each time, he realized that he had taken on too much and quickly reined himself in. "I know it's difficult for you to contract," I told him. "Every cell in you wants to write something huge. And you know, you may just do that someday. But the only way to arrive at that point is to keep thinking small."

Within six months he had completed his article. He had even circulated a draft among his most respected colleagues, whose responses were all positive, and he was well on his way to publication. Then we began talking about what he would write next, once again making certain that he would contain his desire to transform his area of specialization and that he would set his sights on an article of modest proportions. This time we agreed that, instead of tackling an entire issue, he would concentrate on one facet of a larger question, keeping in mind that someday he might well tackle the others.

As well as reducing the amount of time we *think* we should spend writing and focusing our attention on what we *are* writing, thinking small means zooming in on what we plan to write. It means discussing only one facet or element or nuance of a topic, instead of the whole. It means thinking about the memo due next week, not the memo due in two weeks or the report due in a month or our career as a whole. It means considering one at a time the points we need to cover in any one memo, not the memo as a whole. Many writers get stalled at the mere prospect of the book they have in mind. "I don't know where to start," they might say. Or, "I have too much to say." Or, "I'm lost and haven't been able to write for a month."

These complaints are all symptoms of thinking big. I remember peering, as a child, through a pair of binoculars at the base of Mount Evans in Colorado, searching for the summit. Trying to take the entire mountain in through lenses calibrated to telescope long distances, I could see only blurs of green and brown or stretches of blue. Even when someone pointed me in the right direction, my hands could not sustain the focus. Years later what I remember of that mountain is the base camp and lodge where we lived for a month while my father worked with other scientists, measuring cosmic ray intensity. I remember campfires and running in the meadow with the other kids. And a litter of squirming puppies in an old wood bin outside the lodge dining room.

Someone snapped a photograph of me beaming, the pups flop-ping in my lap.

Don't write about the top of the mountain. Write about the puppies. Write about the little girl who loved anything helpless and small. Her eyes too full of the life at hand to turn and take in Mount Evans soaring behind her. Don't sit down to describe the whole mountain, the entire garden, the full day. Don't scare your-self by thinking of the term paper, the essay, or the book. Don't stray into later—tonight, tomorrow, next week, next year. Think small. Hold yourself within the moment. To write your memoir, pick one scene, a single memory. To write a book, launch yourself with one idea, one concept, or one theory. To write a speech, open with single words and phrases. Begin composing one query, not twenty or two hundred. One letter, not three or four or five. Don't write for an afternoon, or even an hour. Write for fifteen minutes today. And then again tomorrow. And tomorrow. Describe one flower, leaf by leaf, petal by petal, filament by fila-ment. Let the leaves and petals, the stamen and filaments, accumu-late, one by one, until you have described it all—the plant and blossom—in exquisite detail. From that single, fully rendered plant, the entire garden will spread before you.

Try This

1. Instead of thinking about *all* the writing you must do—or have not gotten done—think about just one small part. If you are working on a book, focus on the first chapter only. If it's a legal brief, concentrate on the first point you want to make. If this amount of writing feels overwhelming, narrow your sights even more. Think only about the first page or the first paragraph. Then, when you have accomplished your goal, congratulate yourself and negotiate the next small step.

2. Plan your next two weeks of writing by setting aside the same amount of time each day to write. If you have been blocked for a long time, fifteen minutes is the maximum. If you are able to write but often—or always—put it off to the last minute, you may set aside a longer time, but no more than one hour a day. Wait until you have a run of good days before you consider extending your writing time.

3. Try thinking about your writing project as a journey you're planning to take. If you are driving from Philadelphia to Florida, you have to spend at least twenty hours on the road. This seems like a long time, but if you divide the trip into hundred-mile segments, the time appears to pass more quickly. Understand that, each time you sit down to write, you are traveling toward your goal.

4. If you feel overwhelmed by the article, the book or the writing project you want to undertake, try narrowing your topic. Instead of one book, see if you can divide the material into

two or three or even four books, each with a smaller focus. Then, decide which topic interests you the most. If you are writing an article, ask yourself if you are trying to answer too many questions. Isolate the first or the most important question and limit your article to answering just that one. If what you are writing is an essay, remind yourself not to think too far ahead. When you begin, remind yourself that all you are responsible for is writing the piece, one page at a time.

6

Showing Up for Yourself

A few years ago I started teaching a class called *Writing As a Practice*. It's a course I developed after I finished a year of daily walking around a local track and writing about my experience, and realized that the practice had changed my life. Like any new convert I wanted to offer my brand of salvation to the rest of the world. In fact, I was so excited by the unexpected transformation, I would have liked to proclaim my discovery from the rooftops. But because I am a teacher, I proposed a new course instead. It would be a class that helped writing students combine writing with another activity—not necessarily walking—that they engaged in consistently.

The advantages of this plan were clear to me. If we write about something that gives us pleasure, it's likely that the positive feelings will transfer to our writing experience. In addition, writing is a discipline, not unlike meditating or yoga or playing a musical instrument. Combining it with an established practice, one we have already integrated into our schedules, might make it easier to integrate writing into our lives.

I could envision other advantages of dovetailing writing with an additional activity. In my case, for example, physical exercise is beneficial, and writing is my heart's desire. Accomplishing both, each and every day, was a physical, intellectual, emotional, and even a professional boon. After only two months I felt increasingly fit and energized. I also felt productive. I had already written several essays and sensed I would be able to write many more. Of course, I still didn't know in exactly what direction I was headed. Or what the essays I was writing would mean once the year had ended. Still, it was hard to deny that my plan was working on both a physical and material level. Later, looking back on my year, I marveled at how much benefit I had reaped from so small an effort: I felt more fit than I had in years. And I had a manuscript I was pretty certain I could turn into a book. If I could help others tailor my strategy to their lives and passions, perhaps they would experience profound changes as well. All it took was showing them how to combine a practice—any practice—with daily writing, and practitioners would be on their way.

But as I gathered materials for the course and began to examine more closely my own experience, I realized that I had missed the point. Or, if I hadn't missed the point exactly, I had not plumbed my experience deeply enough to perceive its true gold. Sure, exercising and writing daily were useful ends in themselves, leading to increased stamina and pages of output. But in addition to my feeling fit and productive, something more, something immeasurable, had happened in the course of the year: I had become a hero in my own eyes.

Anybody who has ever experienced writing block understands just how astonishing this development was. Frustrated, humiliated, furious at their inability to write, most blocked writers find it difficult not to punish themselves. Far from feeling heroic, they feel defeated and diminished. Ineffectual. They have tried everything in their power—every chastisement, every means of emotional force and blackmail—and they have gotten nowhere. If there is salvation, which many doubt, it is certainly out of their hands, which are condemned to sit idly in their lap.

For many decades of my life, I looked for salvation outside of myself. Until I was well into my twenties, it was my father whom I relied upon to figure things out. Where I should go to college, what courses I should take, where to attend graduate school—he indeed knew all the answers. After my father my then-husband, Barry, assumed the mantle. In those days the world for me was an overwhelming place. Money and finances were beyond my comprehension. Even jobs—the kind you apply and compete for—were outside my ken. Barry marched right in and took charge. He bought and sold our first three houses. He invested our money and followed our investments. When we first moved to Chicago, before I began writing, he sent me out to make contact with the heads of the French department at every local university, in search of a job. "You keep hoping the world will come to you," he told me again and again. "But that's not how it works. You can't spend your days sitting on a park bench waiting to be discovered. You have to go to the world."

Over the years I became more practiced at getting up off my bench. I applied for a job teaching in the freshman English department at Stanford. I became inspired by talking to several Midwestern vegetable gardeners and collaborated with my friend Mary Swander on a book about these gardeners. After my divorce I bought a house. But the truth is, I was never comfortable. Putting myself out in the world the way Barry had urged felt dangerous to me, as if I were dodging bullets. So whenever I could get away with it, I stayed on my park bench.

Then, during my year of walking and writing, something shifted. Something essential. Something so fundamental that, by the end of that year, the world felt like a different place. The bullets had disappeared. The air was clear and fresh. The park bench I had been sitting on most of my life felt claustrophobic. I had started walking, and I didn't want to stop. I wanted to keep going, to stride off the track and into the world. To throw my arms around as much of life as possible. To speak out and have my voice heard, my words ringing clear and true as they floated away from me toward whoever was out there to receive them.

What had happened? Why this revolution within me? Slowly I began to understand, to see that more important than either the walking or the writing was a single and simple fact: For an entire year, I had shown up for myself. Each and every morning, by walking and then writing, I had been present for myself and no one else. I hadn't done this because a friend had asked me to. Or because I was hoping to publish what I wrote. Or because my family expected it of me. My project was more personal and intimate than anything I had ever accomplished in my life. It involved no one other than me: no friends, no family, no teachers. No professors or students. Not even the critics I had struggled with so fiercely throughout college—and still carried within me.

For the first time mine was the only voice I heard as I walked and wrote, my head cleared of the constant babel of the admonitions and demands of others. For the first time I was spending time with myself. And I discovered that I enjoyed these interludes, as well as the company. Every morning the minutes, the hours sped by. Walking, I was like a hummingbird hovering over my own life, sucking the nectar from flowers I was creating by my very presence at the track!

The feeling was not completely new to me. Years earlier, when I was going through a difficult spell, a friend gave me a relaxation tape by Emmet Miller. This was before the explosion in such tapes or the widespread practice of visualization itself, and so I listened very carefully to every word Miller intoned. To this day I remember the thrill I felt, lying on my bed, the late afternoon light streaking across the room, when I heard Miller's voice assuring me, "You have nowhere else to go. Nothing else you have to do."

There it was, permission to let go, to forget everything else I should be doing, everything everybody else wanted me to do. Forget dinner. Forget the laundry. Forget the dog, who would probably love another walk. Forget the friends who were waiting for me to call them back. Nothing was as important at that moment as simply lying there on my bed, listening to Emmet Miller's soothing voice.

"Nothing else you have to do" gave me permission to be precisely where I was at that moment, doing exactly what I was doing. More than permission, Miller's words offered approval as well. *Listen,* the voice seemed to say, *you're important, and what you are doing is important. Don't let anyone tell you otherwise!*

As I prepared to teach my course, I realized that, during my year of walking and writing, I had done for myself what Emmet Miller had done for me that evening many years earlier: I had created a time and a space that belonged uniquely to me. From at least eight to eleven each morning, I granted myself the right to be either at the track walking or at my computer writing. For somebody who had always found it difficult to stake a full claim to her own life, this was a radical shift. No longer was I available to answer the phone, replenish a depleted supply of underwear, scour the kitchen sink, run even the most essential errands. No! As far as the rest of the world was concerned, for two hours every morning I was incommunicado. Not approachable. Off limits! A part of the world, two solid hours, as well as a place—the track—were now mine every morning of the week.

And that was not all. It wasn't only a time and a place I had claimed for my own; I had claimed myself as well. I had carved out a portion of each day to fill with nothing more—or less—than Jane Anne Staw. If not immediately, then slowly, the message hit home: I was important, valuable enough to set aside this time and space for. Valuable enough to say no to anything and anyone else. Valuable enough to honor myself. Simply by scheduling a year-long, 365-day meeting with myself and showing up morning after morning, I rose in my own esteem. Took myself seriously. Began to consider my presence within my own life important.

And there was more. By acknowledging my own importance to myself, by appearing again and again at the time and place I had scheduled, I began to realize how consistently in the past I had walked away from myself, from my own passions and desires. How, the minute anything felt difficult or uncomfortable, I had turned my back and run away, leaving myself in the lurch.

My classes are filled with students who have always wanted to write but haven't been able to. They hope the pressure of the writing workshop will change this, that the structure of a class and the authority of a teacher will help them find the time, the energy, the discipline to write. "With assignments and deadlines, I think I'll be able to write," they tell me. Or, "Knowing you expect me to turn writing in every week will motivate me."

But the truth is, they're wrong. Assignments and deadlines may appear to help, but writing because you are in a class and have assignments is always a Pyrrhic victory. Once the course is over, you'll stop writing. When you take a writing class, instead of focusing on the teacher and the workshop, turn your attention to yourself. Every week, remind yourself that you are in charge of your writing life. That you signed up for the workshop because you decided not only that you want to write but that you have made a commitment to fulfill this desire at a particular time and place. In other words, your presence in the workshop has everything to do with you and very little to do with anybody else.

When they come to see me many of my clients, out of habit or frustration, have reached the stage of self-abandonment. They don't always realize this. Instead, they believe that by making the appointment they are coming to their own rescue, assisting themselves in finding a way out of their block. Or they have decided that something else, something external, is interfering with their ability to write, and that I will help them streamline their lives.

But if I listen to what these clients say about themselves or the way they treat themselves, I know that in their hearts they have already decided they are undeserving of the time and concentration and dedication that it takes to write. To write requires faith in yourself. Requires that you say no to others and yes to yourself. That you believe you are worth standing up for, when deep down you would like nothing more than to walk off into the sunset, to a different life and into the arms of a new and more comfortable self.

One of my clients originally came to see me not because she was blocked but because she wanted help with the direction her writing should take. She had been a journalist and now wanted to cast a wider net and write more features, as well as pieces about her childhood in India, where her father had been a diplomat, and about the death of her sister, with whom she had been very close. For a while I helped her isolate and frame the stories she would write. Then, after she had completed a handful of pieces, she stopped writing. Every piece she started felt futile. "It's not really what I want to write about anymore. I don't feel as if I have anything more to say." So we cast around for other topics. She was a runner, and I quickly suggested she combine her running with writing. At our next session she told me, "You know, I'm just not enjoying running enough these days to write about it." After that we agreed that she would write about music. When that didn't work, we decided on cooking, a lifetime interest of hers. But cooking, no more than her childhood in India, or running or music, engaged her enough to keep her writing.

It was only when my client began canceling her appointments with me that I understood what was happening. For a reason neither she nor I was aware of, she had abandoned herself. While for an entire year she had shown up to write, literally and metaphorically, now she was missing her appointments, canceling her writing time, as if deciding she had nothing to say.

"But I have been *trying* to write," she responded when I told her what I thought had happened. "I tried every day last week. I told you, I just don't have anything to say." When I pointed out that until recently she had plenty to say, she shrugged. "Maybe I've already said it all."

"It's more likely you've denied yourself the permission to speak," I told her. "You may sit down to write, but all the while you tell yourself, 'I have nothing to say. I have nothing to say.' Sitting down to write is one thing. Sitting down with the intention of writing is very different."

To prevent this client from continuing her disappearing act, I suggested she stop trying to write at home and that she only write when she came to see me. For the next several months she spent her appointments with me writing. When she arrived, I gave her a topic to focus on, something simple and straightforward enough that I knew she'd have plenty to write about: "Write about the color red," I might tell her. Or, "Write about the first time you did something like play tennis, eat an ice-cream cone, ride a bike, say no." Or, "Write about milk." Or, "Write about rain."

I soon noticed a pattern in her writing. Whatever she wrote about, her sister, who had been killed in an automobile accident when my client was in junior high school, made an appearance.

Several weeks into this new regime, my client asked if she could take some of what she had written and revise it. "Not yet," I told her.

"Why?" she asked. "I'm finally writing again, and I think I'm getting excited about it. It's only natural that I want to refine it."

"Just wait," I answered. "You're doing everything you need to be doing right now."

"Okay," she agreed.

Several weeks later, at the close of a writing session, she told me she thought she understood what I was doing. "No matter what topic you toss out to me, I write about my sister's death. Maybe I didn't want to think about it, and that's why I stopped writing. By having me write in here every week, you're keeping me from running away from myself and from my life."

Even if we are not writing about ourselves and our own lives, we should place ourselves at the center of our writing lives. After all, if it weren't for us, for our desire to write and our discipline in fulfilling this desire, our words would never find their way onto the page. In the end overcoming writing block involves a paradox. It is by spending too much time thinking too little of ourselves and our talents that we get into this jam in the first place. And it is only by spending enough time respecting—even honoring—ourselves that we can become free to write once again.

If I had any doubts about the importance of showing up for yourself, a conversation I had with my one of my friends convinced me. This friend has been working on her second book for over a year. Recently I asked her how the book was coming along. "I haven't been able to write for the past week. I just haven't had the time. And now, this afternoon, I promised Julie that I'd help her put together the booklets for her poets-in-the-school project. And tomorrow I'm scheduled to help another friend, whose son is in the hospital. And then I'm going away because the partner of my friend Beth in San Francisco has been out of town for two weeks, and I can tell how lonely she's feeling."

"What about you?" I asked.

"What?"

"What about you? You're showing up for everybody else, but in the process it sounds to me as if you're forgetting about yourself, leaving no time for your own thoughts, let alone for writing your book."

"That's an interesting way to put it," she responded.

"Oh?" I said.

"Yes. I know that I run around too much. And I even know I'm too involved with making sure all my friends are happy. But I've never thought about it in terms of not being there for myself."

"Well, are you?" I asked.

"You're right," she said, "I'm not. I can see now that I spend most of my time running out on myself."

"Don't you think you're worth at least some of your time? *I* do!"

"You're right," she said. "I'm going to call Julie and Beth and cancel. I'll tell them I just have to work on my book. They'll understand."

I urged my friend to move a bit more cautiously. Why not wait, and consider showing up for herself the next time she thought of running off to succor one of her friends or neighbors? Instead of worrying about past decisions, she could begin to think about herself and her priorities the next morning, before scheduling appointments. "What's important," I told her, "is to make space to show up for yourself from now on. It's simple."

"Maybe I could tell everyone that I'm on deadline," she suggested.

A deadline involves external force or authority and undermines the benefits of showing up for yourself. Thinking in terms of deadlines lets you abdicate yourself, which is just the opposite of the behavior and attitude you should be moving toward. "It would be better to tell people that, from eight until ten in the morning, you'll be working on your book," I suggested. "Let them—and you—know that this is something you have chosen to do. Simply by repeating that you are writing your book and are not available in the morning, you'll be sending a revolutionary message to yourself. 'I'm important,' you'll be saying. 'Important enough to reserve time and space for myself. Important enough to turn people away. Important enough to count for more than all my friends who may hope for my presence between eight and ten every morning.' "

My friend told me that she couldn't promise results, but that she felt hopeful and optimistic. She had been feeling frenzied and couldn't pinpoint the source. Now she understood that she was uncomfortable not simply because she was too busy, constantly running off to spend time with friends in need, but also because she wasn't leaving any time for herself. "I'm there for everybody else but me. No wonder I feel awful so much of the time. I'm feeling just what I worry my friends will feel if I don't show up for them!"

Showing up for ourselves as writers is both simple and complex. Simple because all it requires is creating time and space for engaging in the writing we aspire to. Complex because without realizing it we are perpetually ducking out on ourselves, disappearing around corners, behind fences, into alleyways and out of sight. *I want to write but have trouble fitting it in. My job is too demanding. I'm always too tired at the end of the day. My children keep interrupting. My desk is too messy.* I no longer see these as excuses for not writing. Instead, I understand that they are all, each and every one, justifications for self-abandonment.

My classes are filled with writers who have gotten into the habit of self-abandonment, always wanting to write but never finding the time or the discipline. They hope I will provide the structure and motivation for them to write. Instead, I tell them, "Make yourself the star. See yourself sitting in this room talking about writing. See yourself reading the writing of other members of the workshop. See yourself with your pen or pencil moving across the page, or the keys of your keyboard clicking."

What I hope is that writers who have had difficulty showing up for themselves in the past will learn to stop leaving their best selves behind when they think about writing. Instead of focusing on externals—the teacher, the class, or a deadline—pay attention to yourself, put yourself back at the center of your writing life. Give yourself credit. You have the desire to write. If you have signed up for a class, you have paid for it with your hard-earned money. You have worked all day, grabbed a bite to eat, traveled to a classroom, and settled into a seat. Be proud of yourself. Repeat as often a necessary, "Hey, I'm doing this. I'm showing up because I want to write. I'm doing everything I can to enable myself to write. I'm on my way."

When I talk to my classes like this, I can feel a shift in the atmosphere of the room. After all, it's seven o'clock, and most of the students have worked a long day and negotiated traffic or public transportation to reach the building in downtown Berkeley where I teach. Some of them have had trouble finding the time or the motivation to write during the past week. Some have written but are unhappy with what they're about to turn in. So there's a tension in the air, as well as stillness. It's as if all the students are holding their breath, trying to remain in their seats and avoid the temptation to split, to run home and plop a pillow over their heads or grab the remote and lose themselves in *L.A. Law.* But as we begin to think of showing up for ourselves, the fog lifts. Spines straighten. Expressions enliven. And within a few minutes the students before me have become three-dimensional, present in body, mind, and spirit. Ready to invest themselves in the next three hours. Ready to talk, to read. And, most important, ready to write.

This is one of the most essential things you can learn about writing: the importance of showing up for yourself. No matter what else you do, clear away the emotional and material time and space—to write. Even if it's just a tiny corner or a quarter of an hour, I hope that you will meet up with yourself there and begin to listen to your voice, making it possible for your own words to find their way onto the page.

Try This

1. Designate a writing time, daily if possible, but at least several times a week, and schedule this time into your calendar or Palm Pilot. To guarantee the time write your own name along with "writing." Then be sure to look at your schedule each morning so that you can see, again and again, your name written into your schedule.

2. When you sit down to write, remind yourself that, for the duration of your writing time, you are in charge of your life. You might even tell yourself, "This is my time. These are my words. These are my thoughts."

3. Think of your writing as a practice, not unlike exercise or meditation or playing an instrument. When you take this perspective, remind yourself that, as you engage in your writing, it is not the product you will be focusing upon but the process. Your writing as product will come into sight later.

4. Begin telling friends and family who ask you to be available to them during your writing time that you are sorry, but no. Tell them, "That is my time to write." Notice how you feel about this response after several weeks.

5. You might spend the first few weeks writing about your feelings. How do you react to seeing that you have made an appointment with yourself to write? How does it feel to be devoting this time to writing? Once you feel comfortable spending your writing time exploring these reactions, you can make the transition to writing about something else.

7

"Real" Writers

I have always been a slow writer. Words do not come easily to me. When I write, I spend a lot of time not writing, trying to come up with the next word, the following idea, the subsequent image. At times I stare off into space, my hands in my lap. Anyone who sees me might not even guess that what I am doing is writing. But it is. I sit and stare; then all of a sudden I know what I want to say and turn back to my keyboard, my hands finding the movement they have been searching for.

For years I was unhappy about the way I wrote, my style as well as my speed. *If I were a real writer,* I thought, *I wouldn't have to work so hard to find my words. Real writers don't feel as if they are slogging through a swamp or trying to see through the soupiest of fogs. Real writers don't look into their heads and see a black hole. A perfectly blank canvas. Real writers' worlds are not literal; for them everything is figurative, made out of material so malleable that it is constantly on the verge of metamorphosing into something else. They see images trotting across a screen; they see metaphors—tea kettles with legs, flowers with wings.*

Of course, the more unhappy I was, the more deprived I felt—and the less able I was to write. I'd try to prime myself by reading my favorite writers, hoping to find a voice in their words. If I could sound like them, I'd be able to write more quickly, more imagistically, more fluidly. Walking in their shadows, I thought I could find my way across and down the page.

Instead, even if I came up with a sentence or two, because I wasn't writing as myself, I'd quickly bump into a wall, any ideas or expressions I had gathered flying in all directions, and I'd be left empty-handed, my mind as blank as when I first sat down. Sometimes the results were even worse. Rather than inspiring me, the writer I was attempting to imitate would offer nothing but discouragement. *I'll never be able to write like that,* I'd think. *Why even try?*

Creating the dichotomy of "real" writers versus "the way I write" is certain to build obstruction between ourselves and the page. In the first place, it makes us immediately feel like frauds. *I'm not a real writer; I'm just a fake.* In the second place, separating writers into two camps, real and not real, immediately distances us from the page. If we think of ourselves as not being real writers, we write at arm's length, with so much space in between what we want to write and what we are actually writing that the distance we have to travel becomes insurmountable. And so much can go wrong along the way!

When I ask the writers in my advanced workshops if they have ever had a problem thinking of themselves as writers, they are quick to respond. "I used to think real writers were more intellectual than I am. I was sure I wasn't a rich enough thinker to write," one woman replied.

"I had a different problem," another writer said. "*Real writers lead interesting lives,* I kept thinking. *Your life is boring. Who will want to read about it?*"

"I used to think that real writers knew exactly where they were headed, but I could never figure out where my stories should end," someone else chimed in.

"My anxiety was just the opposite," a feature writer added. "I always knew where I wanted to end. My problem was knowing where to begin. I thought that real writers never start to write until they can hear the first sentence in their head."

"I used to think real writers never find writing tedious, that they feel perpetually inspired and can't wait to sit down and begin writing," yet another writer admitted. "But if I tried waiting until I was inspired, I'd never write."

There seems to be no limit to the demands we make on ourselves because of notions about so-called real writers. Each of us probably has several sets of expectations. And for all of us, at some time in our writing career, the expectations make trouble—everything from teasing us with our own inadequacy to taunting us about ever trying to write in the first place. The deep message is that, unless we demonstrate a collection of narrowly defined traits, we have never been—nor will we ever be—real writers. Instead, we have been and will remain foolish, mediocre, struggling writers who simply do not have what it takes.

Several years ago a member of one of my workshops told a story about an encounter he had with his mother, who was in the hospital recovering from bypass surgery. The workshop member, who had earned an MBA from a prestigious university, had discovered that he was unhappy working in the world of business, and he decided to realize his lifelong dream of being a writer. "Now is the time," he told himself. "If I don't commit to writing now, I never will." But he had trouble translating his dreams into reality. "No matter how much I wanted to, I couldn't muster the energy to write," he told the workshop. "I didn't feel inspired; I couldn't come up with anything I thought was important enough to write about; my voice was too serious and I wanted to be funny; so I began to question if I was really meant to be a writer."

When this young man went to visit his mother in the hospital, she was lying in bed, her eyes closed, her face pasty, with tubes crisscrossing her body, machines beeping and clicking all around her. "As soon as I walked in, she opened one eye and looked up at me. 'Tell me how you are, Joel.'"

"I told her that I hated my job and had decided to become a writer, but that I was having trouble finding my inspiration and my voice, to say nothing of what, exactly, I was going to write about."

"She listened to what I had to say, then looked me straight in the face and said, 'Joel, writers write. It's that simple.'"

Although I want to fault this mother for her directness, her lack of sympathy for her son's struggle, I have to admit that to a certain extent she was right. Lying there in her hospital bed, a survivor of heart failure struggling to get back on her feet, she was able to cut through all the hype, all the mythology surrounding writers. She didn't care about style or voice, about number of manuscripts completed or the use of metaphor. For her, being a writer was about sitting down and writing. Period.

Perhaps that is why, after Joel told his story, everyone laughed. This didn't mean that many of those laughing weren't struggling just as mightily with the same misconceptions about writers as Joel. Yet they could all recognize that, viewed from a different vantage point, it *is* that simple. People who write can consider themselves writers. And we, the public, consider them writers as well—even though we have no idea under what circumstances and conditions they write. If people write, if they produce articles, stories, novels, book reviews, features, chronicles, we don't ask them to account for the writing process, the quality of their inspiration, or the evolution of their voice before we determine whether or not they are truly writers. This does not mean that we are not interested in the lives of the writers we admire. Or in the particulars of their writing lives. But we label them writers based on their output, not their process or state of mind.

Yet many beginning writers, as well as blocked writers, hold themselves up to ideals they have created from romantic visions or misconceptions about writing. One of my clients said to me, "I can't tell you for how many years I didn't sit down to write unless I felt heightened or jazzed about writing. I assumed that's what writing was all about—perpetual inspiration. It never occurred to me that I could manage to write in any other state. Of course, the more I waited for inspiration, the less often it visited me. That's why I finally came to see you. I hadn't written anything in months."

When I asked this client where she had gotten the idea that writers experience a constant state of euphoria, she didn't know. She couldn't recall ever reading anything of the sort. She had begun writing late in life, and, before that she had paid little attention to what writers wrote about their own writing.

Most of us can't pinpoint the source of our ideas about the lives and processes of published writers. In fact, many people recall reading essays by and interviews with writers that create a very different impression from ease and inspiration: writing is hard work and involves a lot of self-doubt. And still, nearly every one of us has held ourselves up, at some time, to an impossible and impersonal ideal. Each one of us has mandated that our writing take form at a certain pace, in a delimited amount of time, and in a preordained order. And when it didn't, we considered ourselves failures, or nearly so, and we questioned our right to keep writing.

For a reason just as elusive, most of us don't stop trying. Despite our dissatisfaction with ourselves, despite the fact that we fall far short of our ideal, we continue to write. And over time—

whether we begin in the middle or at the end, choose a literal or figurative approach, or feel or don't feel inspired—we come to understand, bit by bit, that the process of writing follows no template. Obeys no rules. Takes place in no fixed or predictable order.

"I had to give myself slack," one workshop member said. "I finally told myself that even if I wasn't profound, I was telling *my* truth and that was important."

"I had a similar experience," a second writer offered. "One day I couldn't stand it anymore—couldn't stand that, every time I tried to write something, I began haranguing myself about how superficial I was. About how real writers always go deep. After all, I'd been a journalist on the staff of a daily newspaper for ten years, and plenty of readers were interested in what I had to say then. Just because I was now writing on my own didn't mean everything had changed. If I was a writer then, I was still a writer, darn it!"

"Me too," echoed another workshop member, who had been working for several years as an editor. "I kept thinking that I wasn't a real writer because I didn't have enough to say. But then I remembered all the helpful comments I gave the authors of the pieces I edited, telling them what was most interesting about their articles and suggesting ways of developing them further, and I realized that, for goodness' sake, I could do the same for myself!"

Some of the writers in my workshops are lucky. When they begin to question themselves—as all writers do—and to worry that they are not real writers, they have past writing or editing experience they can draw on. They are able to stop themselves mid-rant and remind themselves that, even though they may be embarking on a new kind of writing, they are not complete novices. They have enough rope to give themselves some slack.

For me, finding even an inch of play in my rope was harder. I had been blocked for so long, had received so many negative messages about my writing during college, that I had no positive experience to build on. My liberation from the myth of the real writer had to come much more slowly. The first step was contracting with myself to complete one full paragraph of whatever I was writing before I stopped to revise. After a few weeks of this approach, whenever self-doubt began leaking through my determination to write, I had a few polished paragraphs—small successes with which to bolster myself. If I began to think, *No writer writes this slowly,* I could say, "That's okay. You have two, three, four, five . . . paragraphs under your belt. You're writing, aren't you?"

I inched my way along, first counting paragraphs, then pages, and finally entire pieces, all the while reminding myself, "That's okay, Jane Anne. You are a writer. Look, you've written three good pages in the last week. That's something." Later, whenever I began to get stuck, to discount my writing, telling myself once again that I wasn't a real writer, I could correct myself more soundly. "That's not true that you're not a real writer. You've published one essay." Or, "It's okay if this piece is moving slowly. Your last piece did as well, but you finished it. Just write at your own pace."

Over time I continued to write, accumulating words, pages, and essays, and I came to understand that I was indeed a writer. I also understood that real writers are as varied as the books and magazine articles and novels and legal briefs and office memos and dissertations they write. A real writer is anyone who sits

down on a regular basis to write. And for real writers the processes are as different as their personalities. Just as no two people
think or speak alike, no two writers write in the same way. Some
compose slowly, others quickly. Some create the most evocative
of metaphors, while others remain literal, stopping at every red
light, taking no shortcuts, walking only on the sidewalk. Some do
indeed begin in the middle. Others strike out at the end and
grope their way to the opening. Everyone who writes has a different way of going about writing. In part, our success as writers
depends on embracing our own peculiarities. The more time we
spend chastising ourselves, finding flaws in our process, the less
time we have to write.

To accept ourselves as writers, each with a distinctive voice
and process, to identify ourselves as real writers, and to acknowledge our particular mode of composing, we must remind ourselves of small victories along the way. "You might be superficial,
but remember how many responses you received to the article
you published last month. All *those* people consider you a writer,"
one workshop member told herself.

Another sat down one day to read over everything she had
written in the past year. "And you know what I discovered?" she
said. "Even if my writing isn't always profound, the narrator in
each of my stories is somebody I'd like to know."

As we talked, I suggested to another of the workshop members that she correct her misperceptions by taping one of the stories she had written and playing it back to herself each time she
began doubting that she was a real writer. I told the writer who
discounted herself because she never knew where or how to
begin that she should make a scrapbook of the first paragraphs of
her pieces—all of which originally started in the middle—to

remind herself that she never failed to supply what was originally missing.

"What about problems with inspiration?" another writer piped up. "How can I charge myself up for writing when I'm not in the mood?"

Lack of inspiration is a problem for which I don't have a clever solution. Inspiration is not a state we can turn on or off. The word literally means "bringing air into the lungs" and has come to connote a feeling of euphoria. But if we think about the original definition, we can understand that inspiration cannot be manufactured or staged. It cannot be forced. It depends upon the quality of the air we breathe, and we are not always in control of the chemistry of the atmosphere that surrounds us.

We can, however, work to create optimal conditions. To put ourselves in situations where the air is cleaner and clearer, where we are more likely to enter into this altered state. Just as we can travel to the ocean or up into the mountains to clear our lungs of toxic, urban air, we can place ourselves in a state of relaxation before we begin to write.

Several times over the course of a semester, I ask the students in my workshops to sit back, close their eyes, and take a few deep breaths, inhaling completely and releasing any tension as they exhale. "That's right, breathe in and out, in and out, and begin to relax." Once they have taken several cleansing breaths, I help them release all their tension, from head to toe, beginning with their foreheads, allowing the relaxation to travel down past their eyes, their nose, relaxing their mouth and then their jaws. "That's right," I say. "Now your whole head feels relaxed, and you can sense the relaxation spreading down your neck and through your shoulders." In this way they continue relaxing, all the way to the tips of their fingers and their toes.

The relaxation state is important on its own; being relaxed is conducive to writing. But I have another reason for leading these exercises and bringing students into a state of deep relaxation: These states offer a preview of what can happen when you become completely engaged in and absorbed with your writing. When you stop second-guessing and chastising yourself. When you connect completely with the page, leaving no space between you and the words that emerge from you. I am quick to warn that writing doesn't *always* feel this way. Although I have known novelists who told me that whole novels have come to them as they sat by the side of a pool one sunny afternoon, that all they did was place themselves in front of their computers for the next six months and allow the characters and situations to manifest themselves on the screen, my experience of writing is much more like walking up a steep and slippery slope. I write several sentences, then, sliding backward, I delete half of them. This done, I take a deep breath and move perhaps a paragraph or two ahead, then I look up and realize I have no idea where the hill ends. And because I have stopped to gaze upward, I have lost my momentum and begin to slip a sentence or two down. So I stop to gather my forces, then begin to make my way upward again, one sentence at a time, until I am moving too quickly and stumble, sliding an entire paragraph or two downhill.

It is often only when I have been climbing for at least half an hour, huffing and puffing, that things click into place, and the next time I look I have moved a page or two closer to what I think is the crest. Where has the time gone? What have I been thinking? I don't know. For some reason I simply shifted into a different state, becoming one with my body, my feet advancing without my awareness of their movement, my mind no longer noticing each and every step I took, allowing me to move up the mountain more easily than before, without all the conscious effort, the mustering of my forces, the keen concentration. The struggle to move against gravity!

Despite the challenge that writing remains for me, it no longer seems impossible as it once did. Over the past few years I've generated faith in myself and my process. I know that, if I show up and write, something will happen. Now what I remember most about my time spent writing is not the slips and slides downhill, the backtracking, the bruising, but the periods when I have no longer been conscious of every word and each sentence. When, after a slow start, a page or two have flared into shape without my having to strike match after match after match.

This hasn't always been my style. For a long time, when I was blocked, I couldn't create enough momentum to ride a current for even a few seconds. For a long time after that, writing was still a struggle, and although I'm certain I experienced moments of relief, I wasn't yet aware of them. It's only been in the past several years that I have known what it feels like to be carried along by my writing. To feel myself open up to the process enough for the words, the sentences, the paragraphs, and even occasionally the pages to flow. And on top of that to feel my lungs expanding to hold more air, my breath deepening, my heart quickening, so that I feel, quite literally, high, ecstatic. Inspired!

What I've realized as well is that there are no real shortcuts to this state. No strategies for circumventing the time and space needed to sit down and write. We can simulate inspiration. It's an excellent way to get us started when we're feeling anxious and blank. When we've tried sitting down, and nothing seems to come to mind. Or our minds can't seem to settle down and focus. But engineered relaxation doesn't feel the same as writing-induced euphoria. And for that there is no alternative but to sit down and write. And write and write and write.

If you do this, if you sit down each day and write, however little, your writing accumulates. Bit by bit. Sentence by sentence. Page by page. Until you've written one chapter. Then two. And after many months an entire book. There's a simple truth about writing, and it's a truth you have to experience firsthand to grasp completely: Writing produces writing—and more and more writing. There's just no other way. Contrary to all of our expectations, nothing else works to help us collect sentences, paragraphs, pages, articles, stories, memos, briefs, dissertations, and books. No matter how hard we try to think our way into writing. Or to dream our way onto the page. No matter how long we talk or discuss our way into the written word. Or create deadlines and issue ultimatums. Set traps for ourselves. Or punish ourselves. The only strategy that works in the long term is to write. Day after day after day. Week after week. Month after month.

Certainly, if we are blocked and can't write without a great deal of pain and anxiety, we need to discover ways to diminish the pain and make it possible for us to begin to put words on the page. But once we are able to sit down and write, whether for one minute or two each day—or, after many months, for hours each day—the only activity that remains to keep us afloat and writing, to solidify our progress, is the act of writing itself.

A member of one of my workshops compared writing with learning to run. She began jogging with a friend, a veteran of races and marathons. The presence of this friend inspired her, gave her the model she needed to get herself out of bed each morning and to show up at the beginning of the course. Then after a month or so of showing up each day, she called one morning to tell her friend that she had cramps and was going to skip the morning's run. "Not a good idea," he responded. "You need at least to show up and begin running."

"Why?" she asked. "I don't feel good. I won't be able to run for more than a few minutes."

"It doesn't matter," he told her. "You need to begin, and if you can't complete the course, that's fine. What's important is that you keep firing your running neurons. That you not give your body the message that you've stopped running—for any reason."

She discovered that her friend was right. Just showing up and running for a quarter mile helped her jump out of bed the next morning and get going. Later, when she began writing, she remembered her friend's lessons. "Just so I show up every day and write something, even a paragraph, I find it keeps my writing pathways open. That means it's easier for me to show up the next day and the next," she said.

Showing up is a way of gathering momentum. Even the most seasoned writers have some resistance to sitting down to write. There are always other things we might have more fun doing. Or problems that need solving. Or people who need attention. It's only by pushing against these other attractions and demands that we can find our way to our desks, turn our computers on, and begin to write. The more often we write—and it doesn't matter for how long—the more easily we can push through this resistance. Stay away for two days or three, and we have to muscle our way to our desks and our computers, using up energy we could have expended on writing.

Another benefit of firing up our writing neurons each day is that they seem to remain charged even when we're not writing. Write for five days in a row, and then on the sixth day you might sit down and find that the words and paragraphs pour out of you. Without realizing it, without conscious thought, you've continued to write from the time you stopped on the previous day until you sat down on the next day with the intention of writing. What this means is that you are already warmed up, your writing muscles oiled, the circuits of your brain firing. You aren't starting from a complete stop, an absolute standstill. You can take off at a gallop.

Daily writing serves us in other ways as well. A woman in one of my workshops who had put daily writing into practice for several months told the class how different her life seemed. "There's something about the continuity of writing every day that gives my life a shape that feels good," she said. "The daily practice makes me feel more substantial, more important, more present in the world."

Write every day, and your writing grows faster than by simple accumulation. Like a retirement account it will bear interest. We've all seen analyses of what happens when a person invests just five hundred dollars a year over twenty-five years. Because of the accompanying dividends of the account, the amount of money seems to increase by leaps and bounds.

Besides the actual manuscripts—the stories, essays, legal briefs, office memoranda, biographies—we produce by writing, other benefits accrue. Highest on my list is a sense of well-being—the opposite state of mind from the one produced by writing block.

Once we begin to sit down and allow our writing to multiply, no matter what genre we are working in, we feel better. And better. Not only are we no longer behind and frustrated, anxious and embarrassed. Not only do we have pages to turn over to our clients, our boss, our editors, our professors. We have much, much more. We have newfound esteem for ourselves. Esteem because we have struggled and have reached the top of the mountain. Esteem because we are doing what we want and need to do—for our jobs, for our lives, for our happiness.

We might also pocket promotions and raises, tenure and partnership, a BA or Ph.D. We might point to books with our names on their spines on our bookshelves or our coffee tables. We might receive university appointments or fellowships. Win important cases or transform whole departments of our corporation. That all deserves applause. But not one of these advancements penetrates as deeply and spreads its glow as widely over our lives as the sense of well-being we acquire from working our way through writing block.

When I was blocked, hardly a day passed that my block didn't enter my mind. Even when I was engaged in other activities— gardening or hiking, caring for Jonah, preparing elegant meals— whenever I felt a sense of accomplishment, a tiny voice would echo inside my head, "But you can't write."

Many blocked writers have the same experience. Their writing block puts the brakes on feelings of joy and happiness. "Whenever I thought I was having a good time, say at a party," one client told me, "I'd suddenly remember that I hadn't been able to write the report that was due Monday, or the memo that was supposed to have been distributed on Friday, and the icy fingers of panic would grip me."

Another client said, "I could be having a delightful picnic in the country when somebody would mention a book they were reading or an article in a magazine, and boom, I'd be off and running with my anxiety about writing. It seemed that nowhere was safe."

At our first meeting, one of my current clients told me, "I wake up most mornings in a panic about something I've forgotten to turn in, only to realize after a few minutes that I've been dreaming. The only thing I'm responsible for writing now is my dissertation. But I've been so blocked, I haven't even thought about my topic in months." As we talked, we decided that she could ease her way into writing, first by organizing her interview and research notes and writing only one paragraph a day. Quickly, we shifted to a half hour daily. And when that felt comfortable, to one hour. That's all—one hour each and every day. Not more. Not less. The rest of the time my client was free to conduct further interviews, do more research—or just relax. Her dissertation is now more than half-complete. And she told me recently that she couldn't have imagined how happy she would feel.

Sometimes of course, she wishes the writing were progressing more quickly. This writer works by collaging her text, literally cutting and pasting paragraphs together to create a whole. Far from starting with the first paragraph and continuing to write to the end, she thinks about her chapter and writes riffs. Then, once she has accumulated enough riffs, she reads them over and begins to decide how they relate to one another, slowly creating order and continuity out of a bundle of bits and pieces. But at the same time that she would like to write in a more linear way, she realizes that her patchwork method is working for her. That, even if she doesn't walk in a straight line, she can still arrive at

her destination. That, while in the past she might have binged
and sat at her computer for ten straight hours, her hour-a-day
writing is gestating a dissertation, which so far has a beginning
and a middle. And is zigzagging its slow, steady way to a conclusion.

Try This

1. Make a list of the characteristics you expect yourself to have or wish you had as a writer. Do you think writers should write easily? Know when they begin where they will arrive? Use figurative language, filled with metaphors and analogies? Feel inspired all the time? Lead fascinating lives?

2. Reflect on the way you write. Do you get bogged down in the middle of a piece? Do you have trouble beginning? Do you write directly, without metaphors or analogies? Do you lose sight of the end? Do you write slowly, laboriously? Do you have difficulty organizing your thoughts? Finding the right word?

3. Tear up the first list. Most of these characteristics are myths. Now reread the second list, and repeat to yourself—as appropriate—"I am a writer. I may write slowly, with a great deal of difficulty. I may not know where to begin, and I may not create striking metaphors. But I am a writer. I may write slowly. . . ."

4. If you have not begun a daily writing practice, plan to begin one now. Tell yourself that this will be an experiment, that you just want to see if this strategy works for you. Then schedule your writing time for the next two weeks, perhaps for just fifteen minutes a day. At the end of those two weeks, reflect on your experience. Has sitting down to write become less painful? Have you been able to accumulate a quantity of writing in these two weeks?

5. Once you feel comfortable writing for fifteen minutes a
   day, increase your writing time to twenty minutes or a
   half hour. Be careful not to push yourself too far or
   too hard.

8

Choosing Your Reader

Back in the days when I was a blocked writer, struggling with every word I wrestled to the page, I began writing letters to my friends. This was a time before the Internet and e-mail, when high long-distance telephone rates limited communication to local calls and the U.S. mail. Once you went off to college, if you wanted to stay in touch with your friends from high school, you had no choice but to put pen to paper. So I wrote. To my friend Esther at the University of Pennsylvania. To Judy at Connecticut College for Women. To Tina at Wheaton. To my friend Susan at Oberlin. And while my professors and instructors were quick to point out all the flaws in my papers and essays, my friends responded enthusiastically to my letters. "I love receiving mail from you," they told me. "I even read parts of your letters to my mother," my friend Susan said. "I've reread your last letter three times, and it keeps getting better."

I was not unique. I've lost count of the number of blocked writers who tell me that the only thing they feel comfortable writing are letters. They cannot write term papers or tenure articles, law briefs or office memos, but when it comes to sitting down and getting in touch with friends and family, they suddenly discover a fluency that otherwise eludes them. For reasons they cannot explain, writing to people they know well and informally feels like an entirely different activity from any other kind of writing, like running a marathon versus playing tag in a local park. One is fun and energizing; the other is terrifying and enervating.

It was only much later, after years of being blocked and scores of enthusiastic responses to the mail I sent out in my characteristically tiny print, the sentences climbing uphill as I moved down the page, that I began to wonder at the contradiction: If I struggled so to write in college and if I wrote so poorly, why did my friends look forward to my letters? At the time I was much too tormented by my pen-twistedness to take such a long view. The difficulty I had writing in college left me so nearsighted that I had no vision even for the page as a whole. Instead, my line of sight was circumscribed by the single sentence. At times, by the solitary word.

If I had been asked to consider the distance between the response of my professors to my writing and that of my friends, I imagine I would have answered that letter writing wasn't really writing. It was talking to friends and sometimes to family, and none of the rules applied. While in my term papers and in-class essays I tried to prove my intelligence to my professors, I had nothing to prove to my friends. They already knew me, were familiar with my personality, my expression, the ways I thought and felt. They weren't reading to judge my competence or my intelligence. And they certainly weren't reading to give me a grade. The fact that I was writing to them meant I had passed the test long ago. They had already accepted me into their circle, anointing me with their approval.

Not only that, but if they were my friends, we were engaged in a relationship, a give-and-take, a back-and-forth. They could never unilaterally come to a decision about me because of something I wrote. And if they ever did become upset or disillusioned with me, I had the right, in fact the obligation, to respond. I could explain my words, help them see what I really meant by what I said. And set things straight.

How different this was from envisioning Professor Shroeder of the History of Religions department reading my paper on the Old Testament. Professor Shroeder, who stood in front of the lecture hall each week, behind the podium, his baritone voice intoning the Psalms, explicating the origins of the word *gnosis,* quoting Martin Buber, whispering of the "I and Thou." Everything he uttered was enlightened, bathed in the glow of scholarship and erudition. Everything he said was the Truth, to be taken with the utmost seriousness, tucked away in the recesses of my mind, recalled later for a term paper or a final exam.

How to enter into those sacred portals, reach that level of wisdom, articulation, and eloquence? How to find the words and form the sentences to express my own humble ideas? How to tell Professor Shroeder what I was thinking so he wouldn't immediately dismiss me? How to be worthy of this man?

Professor Shroeder was not the only one. There was Heinrich Bölle, also in Religion. And in English, a company of men, all brilliant like my father. All ready to find flaws in my thinking— and in my ways of expressing what I thought.

And how could I even know what it was that I thought, once the tribunal of these men had insinuated itself into my head, sitting in judgment of my every idea? Ensconced in every crenellation of my brain, they were ever ready to pounce. While previously it was my father's voice I heard whenever I considered writing, his critique of my personal essay returning to remind me of my weakness, by my junior year in college I heard a chorus warning me against the dangers of whatever I might intend to express. *Your prose is convoluted. What are you trying to say here? This idea seems sound, but it's buried in confusion. You can't write.*

But *letters* I could write. And I could also write in French. When it came time for me to compose an essay on Verlaine or a term paper on Corneille, the august professors in my head were otherwise occupied, busy with their own scholarship and writing. The minute I stroked an *accent grave* onto the page, the tribunal turned its back on me, their harsh words mutating into the voices of the Pautrat family, at whose knees I had learned to speak French during the summer I was seventeen and lived with them in Paris, in their apartment in the Sixteenth Arrondisement. "La petite americaine," they called me. "Adorable," they said, describing me. "C'est très bien," they often responded when I spoke. When I thought about writing in French, the world went soft for me; it became lyrical, melodic. My throat filled with the fullness of the French *r*, my tongue curved ever so slightly around the *u*, and my lips smiled with the French *oui*. For me French was indeed the world of Baudelaire, the world of *luxe, calme, et volupté*. And within this world, I was chic and articulate.

If I had only known how to combine these two worlds—the world of brilliant academic men and charming, mellifluous French women (for I was mainly with the women of the Pautrat family that summer)—my experience at college might have been different. But again, caught up in the struggle to survive, clinging to each and every English word I typed onto the page in hopes of staying afloat, I could not look up and see the horizon off in the distance ahead of me.

For most blocked writers salvation is possible. But we don't always know ahead of time when or in what form it will appear. Sometimes we meet a professor or make a friend who thinks highly of us and the way we express ourselves. Sometimes we are lucky enough to read a book written in a voice we can identify with—a voice that makes us decide to try again to write because writing in the manner of this author might just be possible. I have even heard of people whose writing careers begin very late in life, after they experience something so profound that they cannot keep themselves from writing. What's important is that we understand writing block for what it is: a temporary obstacle to writing and not a permanent inability to write. The block can be displaced or chiseled away. We simply need to be alert to situations that will help us do so.

For me it was only after I had received my doctorate in French literature and was teaching at a small liberal arts college outside of Chicago that I noticed the first glimmerings of relaxation toward my own writing. And the experience I had at this college was a fluke, an encounter made possible by the logistics of office space.

The college where I taught French language and literature was on a wooded collegiate-Gothic campus north of Chicago, with the Departments of English and Romance Languages housed in a small building where office space was limited. The year I began teaching French, the English department had hired two new assistant professors, one in film and one in creative writing, and the solution to lack of office space had been partitioning off offices in the basement of the building to accommodate the new faculty. So there we were, three young professors, below ground among the boilers and heating ducts, each with a cubicle where we were expected to be available to students for conferences a good many hours per week.

Those were lean years for language study at American universities, and the college where I taught had very few French majors. It was, however, the beginning of the creative writing boom, and a constant stream of undergraduates flowed into Mary Swander's office to discuss with her their fiction and poetry writing. Since the office partitions stopped short of the ceiling, I was able to overhear these discussions of plot, character, imagery, and metaphor, which intrigued me. Mary and her students talked about writing from the inside, from within the story or the poem, while I had been taught to stand at arm's length and gaze at literary technique, theme, and structure from afar. The more I listened, the more intrigued I grew. More than intrigued—hungry. I began to yearn for the kind of intimacy with writing I sensed that Mary had established. But how could I ever find the words to talk about writing with her?

Slowly I began. I don't remember the first questions I asked, but I know that early on I wondered if she could teach me anything about metaphor from the point of view of a writer. I had read Mary's poems and knew that metaphor often lay at the very center of her poems. I, who tended to think either abstractly or literally, seeing only what was before my eyes, wondered what it felt like to write from images instead of ideas, to envision what you were writing about as something concrete.

We began talking, and Mary started showing me the poems she was writing. She even seemed to invite feedback, and then to respect what I had to say. She had a book-length manuscript she was circulating, and although she had won awards and much praise for individual poems, the manuscript was having trouble finding a home. Would I read it and see if I had any suggestions for strengthening it in any way?

The more we talked about Mary's manuscript—the individual poems and the structure of the whole—the more I felt myself wanting to write. Not analyses of the poems of the French poets I was teaching, but poems that had their source within me, at a place I began to sense lay far from the spot where I had always struggled to grab at the words I needed to articulate what was swirling about my head. Then one day, there in the basement of the English and Language Building, in a metal cubicle furnished with a standard-issue metal desk and swivel chair, I remembered that I had written poetry long before I was ever called upon to write exposition. First, in seventh grade, I had composed a poem about autumn, which had been published in a state-wide anthology. And later in high school, under the tutelage of Mrs. Barnes, who had introduced me to e.e. cummings, I had again written poetry, which was again published in an anthology.

Now, I'm certain that, if anyone had ever asked if I had written poetry, I would have replied, "Yes, when I was a kid." For I knew about these poems the way I knew other facts of my life— that I was born in Philadelphia, that I had blue eyes, that my father was a physicist, and so on. I knew all of this as information, because it had been told to me or because I had observed it from without. But that day in my office when I remembered writing poetry in the past, it was a different kind of remembering—a remembering from within, a kind of knowing that has nothing to do with information and everything to do with intuition and sensibility. Perhaps it would be more accurate to say that I *felt* that I had written poetry or that poetry was a part of who I was.

I began to write again, inspired at first by the poems I was teaching my students, and soon after by the world I lived in and my own emotional life. I showed these poems to Mary, who read them and offered feedback. Gentle feedback. Feedback that illuminated what I had set upon the page. "I appreciate the metaphor of 'corners' in this poem," she might respond. "You bring me directly into your experience with it." Or, "I enjoy watching the dust settle from the first stanza of this poem until the last. This helps the poem and the reader move down the page with you."

Listening to Mary talk about my poems, I learned about writing in a whole new way—a way that for me amounted to a revolution. I no longer felt under scrutiny, or even worse, under attack. For the first time I didn't have to tense myself against the sting of criticism, didn't have to hold my breath for fear I would not be able to catch it again once I heard what my reader had to say. Now, instead, I could breathe deeply, from air that was saturated with enough good, clean oxygen for me to fill my lungs again and again. For the first time my words were not used against me, but as conduits to lead me to future words and further poems.

These sessions with Mary in the basement of the English and Romance Languages Building were the beginning of the end of my writing block. The revolution had begun. It was a quiet revolution. It did not involve violence or the immediate overthrow of the ruling party. It did not involve propaganda. Or outward change. It was a revolution that would take years to complete. But it was indeed a revolution, for what had begun as I listened to Mary talking to her students about their writing would continue to work its magic and eventually would completely alter the way I lived.

What paved the way for this revolution, what made it possible for me to sit down and write, free of the block that had tormented me in college, was, in a sense, nothing more than a shift in audience. If in high school and through college I had written for the eyes of my father and his peers, my professors, under the mentorship of Mary Swander, I began writing for a new set of eyes, and rather than intimidation these eyes expressed approval and welcome. Instead of writing toward judgment and criticism, I began writing toward acknowledgment and validation. Instead of writing toward darkness, I began writing toward light.

Most blocked writers are writing for the wrong audience. Blocked, self-condemning, we write for readers who sit in judgment, ready to find fault, to disapprove. Readers who could care less if we finish the novel, the legal brief, the journal article, the op-ed piece in question. We write for readers who don't seem to have much concern for our happiness or fulfillment. Readers who don't see us as full and complex human beings. Readers who have been hanging around for a long time, sometimes invited by us to preside, but more often present via a kind of lèse-majesté, coat-tailed into the tribunal by association or circumstances that have nothing to do with our current life, passions, and goals.

Often, while clients are writing in my office, I interrupt and ask who is reading over their shoulder. If they look puzzled, I explain, "You know, as you're writing, who is reading what you write?" "Oh," they respond, "that's easy. It's my father." "It's my mother." "It's my tenth-grade English teacher."

For most blocked writers there is at least one critic from the past reading over their shoulder. This means that, whenever they write, they are not alone. Instead, they are in hostile territory, where sanctions have been invoked against them. Prohibitions put in place to keep them from accomplishing the very purpose of their visit. And how does it feel to have critics reading every word *as* you write it? "I hate it," most writers will respond. Yet most have never realized previously that they wrote for such a hostile audience.

One of my clients was writing historical fiction. One day she arrived very upset. "I haven't been able to write for the past two weeks. I'm so upset with myself. I thought I had finally gotten a start, but now I'm right back to where I was six months ago."

"No, you're not," I reassured her. "You've hit another snag.

All we have to do is to figure out what's keeping you from writing now."

It takes a while to overcome writing blocks. Since blocks arise from the interaction of multiple factors of personality and circumstance, to unravel them we have to tease apart the various strands. For some writers merely overcoming their initial anxiety about sitting down to write provides a force powerful enough to unravel anything else in their way. For others it is the first step— a step that clears the way just enough for them to bump into the next obstacle they need to work their way through or around.

For this client, who had overcome enough of her block to complete several chapters within a few months, once again bumping into her inability to write felt devastating. By the time she was due to see me, she had dusted off a good many of her old reactions to herself and her writing. "I guess I'm going to be a failure after all," she announced. "It was stupid of me to think I could write this book. Maybe it's just as well. It's probably not any good anyway."

"Whoa," I interrupted. "Instead of digging yourself into a rut, let's see what we can learn about what happened these past weeks."

"That's simple," she answered. "One morning as I began to write, I remembered the first draft being rejected by the publisher, and that was it. I haven't been able to write a word since then."

"Maybe," I said. "But I don't think it's that simple. You've learned to deal with those voices too well. I think something else has come up for you."

Eight years before coming to see me, my client had signed a contract to publish a book. Thrilled, she had worked for a number of years, then sent off a four-hundred-page manuscript full of footnotes and historical documentation. The publisher had rejected the manuscript, telling the writer that what she had turned in didn't resemble the sample chapters of the original proposal, which had been much less academic. Her editor, in a warm and encouraging letter, mentioned my client's talent and urged her to revise.

My client had been devastated by the rejection and had been unable to write for years. But she had never really abandoned her book, whose main character was still very much with her. "I owe it to her to write this book," she told me during our first meeting. And we had focused on her desire to bring to light the life of someone she thought was essential but overlooked in literary history. Remembering her motivation for writing the book in the first place helped my client respond to the negative voices of the publisher that spoke up when she sat down to write. "The first manuscript wasn't really the book I intended to write. For some reason I lost my way. But now I am writing the book I originally anticipated, and I bet you'll be pleased with what I send you."

This new draft was indeed radically different from the version she had submitted to her publisher, and acknowledging this had been an important support for my client in overcoming her block. That was why, when she had found herself once again unable to write, I figured that the recent body block had come from a different direction. To discover more about the complexion of the newest block, I asked her to begin writing, freely, about the morning she could no longer write. I hoped that, as she wrote without censoring herself, she would recover her thoughts and feelings from that moment. I asked her to write for fifteen minutes without stopping, not concerning herself with spelling or punctuation. Or even complete sentences. "Just keep putting words on the page and trust the process," I advised.

A hybrid between full consciousness and a fugue or dream state, this type of free writing often helps us discover what lies just below the surface of our conscious experience. I learned about this mode of writing while I was at the University of Iowa, in a class taught by Paul Diehl. One day Paul asked the students to pick a memory, any memory, however vague, from their childhood. "Now," he said once every one of us had selected a memory, "write into the memory for fifteen minutes. Don't even lift your pen from the page. Just keep writing."

I decided to write about my childhood experience of arriving at my grandparents' Manhattan apartment building for a visit. As I began to write, I felt once again my anticipation as we arrived at West End Avenue and then pulled up to the curb in front of 595, with its green awning and doorman stationed on the left-hand side of the front entrance. Soon I was seeing the face of the doorman, his small chin, his round brown eyes. And then I was walking through the door he held open for me, listening to my Mary Janes tap, tap, tapping as I crossed the tile floor of the lobby and stopped in front of the elevator, which would take me to the third floor and into my grandmother's arms.

It was difficult for me to disengage from my memory when Paul Diehl told the class our time was up. I had waded into a clear mountain lake, and as I floated and swam and dived to the bottom, what was happening on shore seemed less and less important. The water was warm, my body sleek and buoyant; I could stay like this forever.

What I realized once I trudged back to the shore of the classroom and listened to Paul as he talked to the class about memory was that the lake would always be there, accessible if I gave myself the time and space to wade into it. What I also realized was that writing was the path to this lake, that there was something about the focus of writing, combined with the sprawl of the free write, that allowed me to dive deep into these waters and peer at what was swimming below the surface.

When fifteen minutes had passed, I asked my client to read what she had written. "You won't believe this," she told me, shaking her head. "I wrote all about a meeting I once had with my adviser in graduate school. I had begun writing my dissertation, and he told me my committee didn't think I had what it takes to complete my Ph.D."

"You've never told me about this before," I responded. "Do you think about this meeting often?"

"I haven't thought about it for years," she said. "I've thought the publisher rejecting my book manuscript was what made me feel like such a failure. Now I wonder whether that rejection just intensified my failure as a graduate student."

"You're probably right," I said. "Your adviser's comments functioned like a magnet for the rejection of your book, giving the words of your publisher even more clout than they might otherwise have had."

"Of course," she replied. "If I hadn't had the bad experience in graduate school, what they said about my book might not have felt so devastating."

"And remember what they said."

"That my book was nothing like the proposal they had read; it was much more academic."

"Now do you have a sense of why your book might have sounded too academic?" I asked.

My client cocked her head, waiting for me to answer my own question.

"Is it possible that you wrote the book to prove to your adviser and your committee that they were wrong, that you were indeed capable of writing your dissertation?"

My client and I went on to talk about audience—the reader or readers she thought she was writing for. By the time she left my office, it was clear that she had written the first manuscript, the book the publisher considered too academic, with her graduate adviser in mind. Not that she was conscious of the audience she had chosen. She thought she was writing for her editor and her publisher. For her future readers. But as a result of dropping out of graduate school, she had a great deal of unfinished business she was trying to resolve. Publishing a book with a prestigious New York press would certainly silence those academic voices once and for all.

When she came to see me initially, my client and I had worked only with the voice of her publisher, finding ways for her to respond to the publisher's criticism and rejection. Having responses at hand for the voices the publisher and editor sent her way allowed my client to begin rewriting her manuscript. However, she had never really dealt with the academic audience, her equivalent of the professorial tribunal that discouraged my writing for so many years. And after granting her a brief respite, the academic audience had once again emerged, flagging her down and pulling her to the side of the road.

It didn't take much for my client to incorporate a more positive reader into her writing life. Affirming that she still felt she owed it to the subject of her book to complete her project, she invited this historical figure to be her sole reader. Because she still associated the publisher with criticism, she realized it would be better to banish them from her writing room while she worked. At the same time she explained to the academic tribunal that she no longer needed their approval; she had moved on; her goals and her writing had evolved; she was writing a trade book, not a dissertation.

Each of us has an ideal reader. And this reader is not always the same. Depending upon what it is we are writing, we can envision various audiences, readers with whom our relationship is quite different. Often we have these readers in mind without being conscious of their presence, and it is only when we tease them into the full light of day that we realize they have been reading over our shoulders as we write, commenting, judging, approving—or, if we are blocked, disapproving—of every word, even every comma we commit to the page. That is why, as a blocked writer in college and beyond, I was free to write entertaining letters to my friends. When I sat down and penned, "Dear Susan," I shut the door on the professors who blocked me, and instead I looked out on the smiling face of my best friend. Or, when I wrote with fluidity and grace in French, it was an image of the Pautrats I held in my mind's eye. It was for them I wrote about the plays of Corneille and the poems of Valéry. It was their heads nodding and encouraging me that I held close as I wrote. And later, when I once again began composing poems, it was so my friend Mary Swander could read them. At the same time I also wrote for Miss Barnes, who had applauded the poems I wrote in high school.

It does not matter who this ideal reader is. What matters is that we write for eyes that approve of us. Eyes that we respect, but that also look upon us kindly, lovingly. Eyes that have not spoken

to us harshly. That have not disapproved of us. Eyes that encourage us. Eyes that want for us what is best.

Once my client understood that she had been writing for the
wrong audience, she was able to resolve the humiliation she had
felt as a graduate student and to purge her adviser from her writing life. "I can't be that incapable," she reasoned. "The publisher
gave me a contract and an advance. They loved my proposal." She
also understood why her editor had rejected the first manuscript.
"I had written that book to prove something to my graduate
adviser, not to fulfill the contract I had with the publisher. No
wonder they were disappointed!"

Discussing her ideal reader, my client realized that this reader
was the reason she was writing the book in the first place. An
underappreciated writer whose genius my client had discovered,
this figure was in some ways quite similar to my client. "If I consider her my reader, we will be helping each other. I'll be bringing her talent to the light, and she'll be helping me write. It's a
win–win situation."

By chance I discovered my ideal reader in Mary Swander. We
all have encountered ideal readers at some time or another—a
former teacher, a college roommate, a sister or a brother, a cousin,
an aunt, a next-door neighbor, a lover. It may be someone we
have been out of touch with for a while or someone who is very
present in our current lives. To write for these ideal readers, we
must first ferret out those readers who stand in the way of our
writing and ask them to leave. Then we are free to invite our
ideal reader into our hearts and minds as we sit down to put
our words onto the page. In my experience these ideal readers
never refuse. They are always eager to lend their support to the
important business of writing. Rain or shine, morning, noon, or
night, they will be there, beckoning the writer, sustaining and

embracing the writer through all the excitement and hesitations of the writing life. All we, as writers, have to do is to let them know we need them. And from time to time to thank them for lending themselves to us in such an important and productive way.

Try This

1. Write a short letter to three different friends about some- thing that has happened to you recently—a good movie you have seen, a trip you have taken, a lecture you have attended, something amusing you have witnessed. As you write, notice how you feel about writing to these three people. Do you feel most relaxed with one of them? Does the writing flow more easily when you visualize one friend rather than another? Do you look forward to writ- ing to any of them?

2. If you felt most comfortable writing to one of the three friends you selected, write a letter to that friend about the report, the story, the dissertation chapter, the legal brief you have been putting off writing. Begin "Dear So and So," and tell the addressee that you are writing to explain your theory, plot, logic—whatever is appropriate—for something you have had difficulty writing.

3. Choose a memory—a vague memory actually works best— and begin writing about it. You can do this by selecting one detail and writing down everything that comes to mind asso- ciated with this detail. Continue writing for fifteen minutes without stopping. Try not to lift your pen from the page and don't try to write grammatically or even in full sentences. If you are surprised at how much you have to say about this memory, try the same strategy with the writing you have been delaying. Select one detail and then continue to write for fifteen minutes without stopping. Once again, put ques-

tions of grammar and syntax out of your mind. There will be time to review these elements later. The goal now is simply to discover what you know or to uncover what has until now remain submerged.

9

Making Your Writing World Even Safer

One of my clients was having a difficult time writing. In fact, it had been several months since she had written a word. Yet I knew that, once she sat down, her hand could fly across the page. I had seen this happen during our appointments, whenever I asked her to take out her pen and capture in her notebook a story or an image she had just presented orally. Determined to break her nonwriting streak, I invited my client to come to my office each morning and spend an hour writing with me. I was confident that, if I could engage her consistently with her writing, she would accumulate a savings account of positive experiences—in addition to several publishable pieces.

She agreed to give the plan a try and showed up the following Monday at nine-thirty, notebook and pen in hand. We talked briefly about a story she had told me the previous week, an adventure she and her older brother had with a Barbie doll when they were kids, and we agreed that it was worth writing. Quickly her pen made contact with the page, and every morning for the next few weeks, she leaned back into the love seat in my office, in front of the French doors facing my garden, while I sat at my computer, the *click, click, click* of my keyboard harmonizing with the *scritch, scritch, scritch* of her pen. Each day she began by reading to me the last page from her previous day's writing and closed by reading me all that she had written that morning. Near the end of the second week, when she had nearly completed her first story, she told me that she had reflected a lot about what was happening in my office and that she thought she understood her problem.

"I don't feel safe writing by myself. I don't understand why; I just know now that I never felt safe. But somehow, in here with you, the two of us writing together, I'm no longer afraid."

The place you write may be an important safety factor for your writing. One of my friends writes best outdoors, preferably by a creek. The trilling birds, the rushing water, put her mind to rest. The minute she comes indoors, into her "office," she begins to place unrealistic demands on her writing. By the creek she is able to tap into the harmony of the natural world, open to the way everything—trees, water, squirrels, caterpillars—is part of a larger whole. Within this context nothing she writes can matter enough to incite panic.

Some of my younger students work best at cafés. At a table their laptops open in front of them, a latte by their right hand, they write. These writers don't need silence. Street noises from outside wafting in, snippets of conversation floating through the air, the swish of the espresso machines all create a symphony of safety for them. For these writers life needs to feel full of possibility. Sitting in a café, with writers, students, friends, and strangers surrounding them, they do not suffer from the deprivation of a lonely apartment. They are out in the world, not missing out. This is the electric situation they need to write.

Often students in my U. C. Extension classes find safety after-hours at work. Knowing that the office space is finally all theirs, as well as the time, that no one will approach with work for them to do or questions for them to answer, provides just the atmosphere of freedom they need to write. "It's as if I'm writing at work and getting away with something," a student once told the workshop. "Usually when I'm sitting in front of my computer, I'm writing for my company. That's why it feels so good to be using the same computer, writing for myself."

"I agree," another student echoed. "But I prefer going in early in the morning, before work begins. I love the feeling of being the first one in the office. It's a way of staking out my psychic territory, and the words come pouring onto the page."

The place, or the space, where we write is important for several reasons. No matter what its particular texture, every writer's block originates in fear. Something about writing—and this something is often unique and personal—does not feel safe. Although many of the factors that contribute to our feelings of unease are intangible, place is not. Whether it involves four walls, a ceiling and a floor, or a sky overhead and the ground beneath us, the actual space in which we place ourselves to write is physical, and because it is physical, we have the power to shape it according to our standards of safety.

In addition to contributing to our sense of physical and emotional safety, the place where we write can infuse us with a sense of aesthetic well-being. Writing is always an expression of who we are. If it does not communicate and capture all of our complexity, it always articulates at least a part of our personality. When what surrounds us as we sit down to write clashes with our character, with what we perceive to be harmonious or pleasing to our senses, we feel tense—often without being aware of why—and it becomes that much more difficult to capture words on the page.

A writer I am working with created a home office for her writing. Having two small children, she needed to find a place where she could step out of her role of Mama and into that of writer. But no matter what she did, no matter what changes she made in this home office—moving her desk in front of the window that overlooked her garden, buying a new reading lamp—she didn't feel comfortable writing in this room. Desperate, one day she told her baby-sitter that she was leaving for an hour, and she drove over to her consulting office. It was a Saturday, so my client had the office—the entire building, in fact—to herself. And she found that there, seated at her desk, piles of work paper rising around her, she was able to complete an article she had been struggling with for quite some time.

"I don't know exactly why this happened," she said the next time we met. "I would have expected that sitting at my workaday desk would have put me in a state the opposite of inspiration."

As we talked further about her experience of writing at her workplace, we began to understand. "How do you feel at work?" I asked.

"I feel competent. I know that I'm good at what I do and that I come up with creative solutions to the problems I'm given to solve."

"And how do you feel when you sit down to write?" I asked.

"Exactly the opposite," she replied.

"So?" I said, waiting for her to react to what she had just said.

"Oh, I see! If I sit at my consulting desk to write, I can borrow some of my competence as a professional to help me."

It is understandable that for new or blocked writers the world of their professional life—a world where they are highly regarded, where they have forged a sense of competence and efficacy for themselves—would offer the aura of safety absent from their writing world. By leaving her house, where she felt like a harried young mother, and driving to her office, where she could claim her identity as a respected professional, my client was able to sit down and write without all the doubts and hesitations that assailed her at home.

Safety for writers means many different things. For all of us it means putting a stop to the name-calling so many blocked writers engage in. For all of us safety also means softening the demands we place upon ourselves when we sit down to write, creating an atmosphere where we feel safe enough to take the kind of risks involved in finding the words that dwell within us—some in the deepest recesses of our hearts and minds—and exposing those words to the light of the world outside ourselves.

It is in ensuring our safety as writers within our own world that we can tailor our writing situation and context to our particular needs. The client I invited to write with me in the morning discovered that solitary writing left her feeling vulnerable and that my presence was protective. Another of my clients found companionship in simply knowing that she and her friend, who lived some distance away, were at their computers at the same time each morning. During a period when neither was writing as regularly as they wanted, they agreed to call each other at nine o'clock each morning and speak of where they had stopped writing the previous day and where they intended to begin that morning. Then they hung up and continued to tell their stories on the screen, the afterglow of the conversation lighting the air around them.

Writing is a solitary business. Imagine, then, how much lonelier it feels when as writers we abandon ourselves, when we become angry at our hesitations and stutterings, and turn against ourselves with name-calling and accusations. The presence of another writer in the room can not only ward off any sense of danger, it can also protect us from our most vicious attacks against ourselves. When I invited a second client to join the morning writing sessions, she was thrilled. "That way I won't be able to yell at myself all the time when I write," she said. "I can't keep calling out, 'You're stupid!' with other people in the room."

I am more private than many of my clients. Sharing my writing space with other writers is only a recent possibility for me. In the past I needed almost complete solitude to write. There were times that even knowing someone else was in the house disturbed my writing. A footstep, a cough, a throat clearing were enough to break the amniotic sac I needed to bathe in.

Now that the cord between me and my writing is strong enough to support my emotions and my words, I no longer require absolute privacy when I write, though I still prefer it. Years ago, when a friend who took a job at a distant college bequeathed his library carrel to me, I discovered that this was a perfect environment in which to write. In a small room on the third floor of a university library, on the edge of the stacks, windows facing outward to the campus, I could write without disturbance. At the same time I was not alone. Students and other writers kept me company, browsing in the stacks, sitting at their own desks, in front of their typewriters, their words taking shape down the page, our silent community coalescing through the walls, syllables, sentences, paragraphs, ideas, and images dancing invisibly in the air around us.

By the time I invited my client to write with me in the morning, I had discovered other safety measures for my own writing, as well as for the writing of other clients. That is what my work is all about: helping writers make every nook and cranny of their writing world safe. The physical situation in which we write is one of the many factors we can personalize. It's a bit like creating a fort for ourselves, armed not with weapons but with physical and emotional comforts that make us feel secure. Photographs of close friends, our partner, or our children can contribute to this sense of fullness and safety. I once asked a client who was having a very difficult time being kind to herself to buy a bouquet from the local florist each week. Seeing the vase filled with her favorite flowers on her desk when she sat down to write not only reminded her to be more gentle with herself, it also made her feel less vulnerable to attack. "I feel as if something of beauty is standing guard by my side," she told me.

A beautiful rug, a painting, a framed poem by your favorite poet—any of these can help transform an ordinary, everyday place into a writing space—an area lifted out of the quotidian, away from the complications and cares of our lives. Once we are fully unblocked, this is just where our writing can take us. Until that time, props can help ease the transition from the world to the page, from anxiety and vulnerability to relaxation and inspiration.

Safety can also be assured by the cooperation of our friends and family in legitimizing the space or the span of time in which we write. Turning off the telephone and keeping the outside world away while you write might create just the degree of safety you need. For writers who find writing a lonely business, the ringing of a phone they do not answer helps them feel connected to a world from which they remove themselves to write. One of my clients was very social, her free time filled with lunch dates, excursions to plays, museums, and concerts, hikes with friends, travel to Europe. As we worked together, she realized that, each time she went into her office to write, she felt forgotten by the world. Abandoned by her friends. "It's ridiculous," she told me, "but whenever I sit myself down to write, I think everybody is getting together to have fun. I feel terribly left out."

"I know how you feel," I told her. "My phone used to ring often, with friends wanting to spend time with me. When I decided to write every day, I had less free time, and the phone stopped ringing. Before I realized that I had *chosen* my writing over lunch dates, I felt abandoned."

To ease this client's sense of isolation, I suggested she ask her friends to leave her supportive messages on her answering machine during her writing period each day. "Hi, Joanne. Just wanted you to know I'm thinking of you." "I was wondering if you'd like to go for a walk this afternoon." "I look forward to hearing what you write about today." Greeted by these messages when she finished writing, my client no longer felt the keen sense of isolation that had troubled her before.

Once they have found a safe writing space and they begin to write, some writers have trouble knowing how to stop or where to procede. To clients who can't let go of their writing, or, who, even when they do write, tend to beat up on themselves for not having written enough or brilliantly, I have suggested mailing off each day's pages to me as soon as they finish a writing session. "Just print it out or fold it up and stick it into an envelope with my address." By sending their daily pages off in an envelope addressed to me, they put the ball in my court. If they begin to question their work or criticize themselves, they have an immediate response: "It's no longer my problem. Let Jane Anne worry about it." Once every few weeks the clients and I review the writing I have received, and together we decide what they will do with it.

I once worked with a marketing specialist who was writing a book on advertising. He could type a first draft with ease, but after the words were printed out in hard copy, he could not bring himself to the revision phase. Again and again we talked about his difficulty, wondering why taking what he had written the first time and beginning to shape it into its final form seemed so daunting. One day I asked him to bring his disk to my office, and he watched while I began to revise his work. "What does it feel like when I delete a paragraph or move an idea to another page?" I asked.

"It feels cruel to me," he answered, "as if you are abandoning a part of me."

I suggested that in the future, when he began to revise, he do so on a second copy of his first draft. That way he would no longer be losing part of his original creation, and as a result the revision process might feel safer.

Writers who have difficulty violating the integrity of their first draft may find it helpful to create a new file for the remnants of their original writing. "I'm always terrified of deleting the wrong thing or throwing away something I will need later. Making a backup file of my deletions brings my worry factor way down," one client told me. Another realized that, by cutting out or rearranging what he had first written, he felt as if he were betraying himself. "It's as if I'm telling myself that what I wrote the first time wasn't any good, and that feels terrible. By transferring my deletions to another file, I am not discarding; I'm actually saving a passage for future use."

It is understandable that some of us have difficulty with revision. After all, our writing is an expression of who we are, capturing on the page what we think and feel and the way we see the world. Because we naturally identify with our writing, revising it can feel like self-criticism. It's as if we are telling ourselves that we're not good enough, that we're in need of refinement or additional support. I have often heard new writers remark that deleting their own words feels as if they were cutting off an arm or a leg.

Our closeness can also make it difficult to see what about our writing could be improved. I have worked with clients who wonder why they can help other writers but not themselves. "If this were not my own essay, but somebody else's, I would probably be telling them exactly what you're telling me. Why can't I do this for myself?" they ask.

Because you see your writing from the inside. These are your thoughts, your words, your images, and you're intimate with them as soon as they land on the page. What you read is familiar, what you expect to read. What you see on the page is the way it is supposed to be. Each word in its place, each thought given precisely the right amount of space to express itself. This makes revision nearly impossible.

Reading your own writing can be like viewing a painting from only a foot or two away. You may see some brush strokes more distinctly. Certain lines more intensely. But you have no sense of the whole. However, while to take in more of the canvas, we simply have to step back several feet and look again, achieving the same perspective on our writing may be more of a struggle. To help myself create the distance—and the safety—I needed in order to revise my first book, I hired a reader. She came to my house every afternoon and read one chapter aloud. Hearing my words in a different voice allowed me to let go of what I had written, to relinquish ownership. To listen more objectively to what was being read. When my own words came toward me, traveling over the airwaves, they were no longer an integral part of me, and I didn't feel defensive or have to struggle when they needed revision or cutting.

The client who wrote with me each morning for several months is now writing in her office at home. By the time we discussed the transition, she had completed several stories. But before she was ready to make the move, she wanted to revitalize her office, ridding it of clutter, organizing her files, emptying the space of any artifacts that might discourage her from writing. Years earlier she had pursued a different career, and since that career was in her past, and writing was in her present and future, she no longer wanted to be surrounded by what she used to do. "When I return home, I want everything in my environment to be compatible with writing."

This client and I still work together, although now we only meet every two weeks to review what she has written and to help her enter what she plans to write next. "Do you know what story you want to tell now?" I might ask. And if she's already decided, she talks to me about her next piece, briefly narrating the plot and explaining why she thinks it will work on the page. If she doesn't know what she wants to write, I ask her to tell me a story. As she talks, I listen, hard, to see if I think this tale will eventually make for good reading. If it will, we discuss where she might begin. What's at stake. What the main twists and turns of the story are. And knowing that she has my vote of confidence for the story she plans to tell wards off this client's panic about writing. "When I have your blessing, I don't become terrified one or two or even ten pages into whatever I'm writing and begin to worry that it's no good, that I don't know where I'm going, that I should never have decided to write this story in the first place. I feel as if I have a protective shield around me when I write—a shield that keeps my doubting and critical self from entering."

I might never have understood fully just how important all aspects of the safety factor are for writing if my husband, Steve, hadn't built me an office in the backyard. Ten years ago, when I bought the house, an old redwood potting shed listed toward the fence at the back of the property. I used the space not only for gardening paraphernalia but also for storing extra chairs, bikes, and anything else I couldn't fit into my tiny basement. Before Steve and I combined households, I had outfitted a downstairs bedroom as my office. With bookshelves lining the walls, a love seat against one wall, and a Persian carpet on the floor, I was pleased with the look and feel of the place and enjoyed meeting with clients and writing there.

Then we needed a guest room, and Steve offered to transform the potting shed into a new office for me. When the room was completed, I knew immediately that it was an aesthetic success—vertical redwood siding, a pitched roof, two sets of French doors opening onto my garden, bookshelves along the entire back wall. But once I settled into working in my transformed potting shed, I was aware of an important emotional shift as well. Although I had never felt uncomfortable in my old office, I was pervaded by a sense of complete well-being whenever I set foot into my new space. Within its walls, looking out on my perennial bed to my left, a portrait Steve painted on the large wall to my right, I felt freer, looser, more optimistic than ever before. *This is my space, my space, my space,* every surface whispered to me.

I still feel euphoric about this office. Everything in here is mine, from the Chinese scroll on the wall near one set of French doors and the three ceramic pots on the shelf to the collection of figurines in a corner of my desk. It is mine, for me to use and to give me pleasure. It is mine, and it is complete in itself, not just one room in a house of living room, dining room, kitchen, and three bedrooms. Not just one room in a house inhabited by others. Not just one room on the way to any other rooms. Even more than safe, in my office I feel complete. There is nothing else I want and nowhere else I want to be.

Of course, not everyone is lucky enough to live with a carpenter and own a home with a dilapidated shed. But had I known what I know now, I could have made changes in my old office that might have made my writing world even safer. I might have reconfigured the furnishings, moved my desk to a different part of the room. Changed the curtains on the windows. I might have created an alcove and designated it my writing space. Divided the room in half with bookcases. Bought a Japanese screen to provide additional privacy when I wrote or to establish an area of invisibility around my desk.

Even those writers who feel they have little difficulty getting words onto the page may find ways to make their writing world safer. Writing involves a complex relationship between writers and their surroundings. For us to be fully fluent as writers, to access all parts of ourself and all of our selves, we need to make our writing world foolproof. To do all within our power to help us feel completely at ease, protected from interruptions, insults, distractions, demands, and unhappiness. To work with ourselves, our family and friends, our environment so that nothing comes between us and our ability to express ourselves on the page.

Try This

1. Try writing in several different locations, both within your home and outside, at cafés or in public parks. Notice how you feel in each setting; where you feel most relaxed and fluent; where you feel most constrained.

2. If you do not have a room of your own, personalize your writing space with photos, paintings, flowers, a beautiful rug. If you write in a public space within your home—in the kitchen or a corner of the living room—you might buy a screen to place behind you to create a sense of privacy.

3. Create a writing partnership with a friend, agreeing that you will both write each day at a certain time. You might phone each other just before you begin and then again when your writing time is up, taking each conversation as an opportunity to discuss your feelings about writing. Or you can touch base before you write, then e-mail your installment to each other when you finish writing every day.

4. Invite a friend to write with you several times a week, either at your home or your friend's. You might set aside fifteen minutes for conversation, then lead into your writing session with a short meditation or relaxation, with the understanding that once you start writing, conversation stops. If this seems too rigid, you might decide that at certain intervals you will read to each other what you have written. Or you might agree to coach each other through moments of difficulty. One productive strategy for accom-

plishing this is to read the sentence or sentences in question and ask for feedback. Often another writer will know whether you should simply continue writing or begin again several sentences earlier.

10

The Peace Process

Most of the blocked writers I work with have been at war with themselves for quite some time before they call me, so our first meetings usually focus on declaring a truce and making certain they understand the conditions of this truce. First we stop the name-calling. Next we discuss the provisions necessary to maintain the truce. In order not to wage war against ourselves as writers, we need to learn how to promote and sustain an atmosphere of peace. How can we live with ourselves so the tension doesn't mount as the days pass? How can we continue to write without being disappointed in ourselves, without escalating our demands or feeling frustrated that we have not yet completely eliminated the reason we went to war in the first place? Or without fearing that war will break out again in the future?

Think about it. If the Israelis and the Palestinians are ever to remain at peace, they will have to learn to live together, side by side, perhaps even in the territories of the West Bank, in towns and villages that were once all Arab or entirely Israeli. With the habit of hostility and suspicion conditioned by their differences for the past sixty years, this will take time. Even if Arafat and Sharon shake hands over a treaty they both endorse, it will be years before the air is filled with peace. Peace will be a process, as well as a product.

The same is true of overcoming writing block. It is a process that takes time. And one of the best ways to ensure the end result we seek is to understand that writing itself is a process, not a product. Most people who have difficulty with their writing do not realize this. They do not realize that writing takes place over time, in a series of stages, each with its own particular focus. For years I did not know this. And that was one of the reasons I became so tangled in each and every sentence I typed onto the page. I thought everything I wrote should be perfect the first time. Should sound elegant as well as contain its full quota of information. With every comma and semicolon in place and every word correctly spelled. So many ends to be fulfilled, all at the same time. So many responsibilities, each requiring different rooms of my intelligence. Different doors to be opened and closed. Trying to accomplish them all simultaneously was impossible.

Because I didn't know this, didn't know to tease apart the various ends and deal with them consecutively, one at a time, I wrote and rewrote and rewrote again and again each and every sentence. It was many years before I entered fully into the process of writing, realizing that I could—and should—limit my focus to one goal at a time. Now, as soon as new clients come to see me, I initiate them into this process-approach to writing. "The first time around, all you are responsible for is capturing your ideas on the page. Ideas, not logic or punctuation or elegance of phrase or spelling. Just ideas, ma'am, nothing but ideas," I emphasize.

Once we embrace idea-generation as the first stage of the writing process, we find that the fist of anxiety in our stomach begins to relax. There is no longer as much at stake with every writing effort. We don't need to be good spellers and thinkers and grammarians and speakers all at the same time. As we write, we can don these hats in succession, taking each off the shelf then replacing it until later when we need to wear it again. No more juggling. No worrying about keeping everything in the air at once. No frenetic movement to grab hold, then quickly relaunch, over and over. Just one hat at a time, placed solidly on our heads, with no danger of slipping off.

As writers settle into this more relaxed state at the outset of writing, they notice their mind traveling to new and exciting destinations. No longer worried about taking care of so much business at each sitting, they are at last unfettered, free for the first time to journey to parts of their mind they may not have visited in quite some time. Bit by bit their thoughts wander both farther away from and deeper into the topic at hand. This is the phase of writing as discovery, a time when many writers happen upon what it is they really want to say. Even if they set out with an itinerary in mind, they might make an unplanned stop, take what they think is a wrong turn but reveals itself to be an exciting stopping point, or become intrigued with a town they thought they were going to drive quickly through. Other writers begin their trip having settled on a final destination only, their route uncharted, intending to wander freely as they make their way to the large X on their map, where their journey will end.

A few writers even set out without a clear destination. They may not know where they want to land, only that they want to journey in and around a general area. Perhaps it is the Southwest or New England. The Rocky Mountains. Or the state of California. And they set out, eyes, ears, and other senses open to whatever they wander into, their only limitations the size of the state or geographical area they have targeted before leaving home. This mind-set allows us to relinquish control of our writing during this initial stage. It helps us learn to trust that the process of writing itself will lead us somewhere. This is why writing teachers often use "free writes" in their classes. "Write about the color blue," a workshop leader may say. Or, "Write about tears." Or, "Write about your favorite food." Or, "Begin with the following sentence and then write for fifteen minutes without stopping: *When I was ten, what made me happiest was. . . .*"

Free writes help new writers see how much they actually have to say, and also demonstrate to them how easy it is to find their way on the page. Of course, writing this way routinely—with no travel plan, not even any maps—is only for the bravest or most experienced souls. Most of us work a middle ground, with a flexible itinerary and several stopping points in mind before we actually begin, understanding that we are open to, even invite, discovery along the way. With the opposite mind-set, writers who spend days or weeks creating elaborate outlines easily run into trouble. If nothing else, how can writing be pleasurable if you have no time to take advantage of unforeseen opportunities? If the minute you begin, you have eyes only for the end and deny yourself glances to the left or right of the highway?

That is why, when clients tell me that their writing problem would be solved if only they could create an outline fine-tuned enough to point out exactly where they need to go, I worry. In my experience outlining to excess is an impediment rather than a facilitation to writing. A way of postponing actually sitting down to write. Of not facing our difficulties and instead seeking stop-gap strategies for overcoming them.

At this stage of writing-as-discovery, anytime you begin to seize up, to worry about the details of writing, you can remind yourself that you are not yet responsible for the way the sentences articulate themselves or the way the words are spelled. "Just ideas ma'am, just ideas." And at long last you can refrain from constantly repositioning the cursor at the top left-hand side of the page, refrain from stopping in order to figure out where to begin for the fourth, fifth, sixth time. Or how best to formulate an idea. Or to compose a sentence. Now, perhaps for the first time in your life, you can write. And continue to write for some time, without stopping.

After you catch on to this first, writing-as-discovery stage of the process, you move on to the second phase: concentrating on organizing your ideas, fashioning a logic for your argument or a chronology for your narrative. Now you can draw arrows from one page to another, cut and paste, renumber paragraphs to create a more convincing order, make the second paragraph the fifth, the first the conclusion, eliminate the seventh altogether. If some— even many—of your sentences sound awkward or monotonous, never mind. That responsibility comes later.

With the flow of the piece established—the path the writing takes from the beginning, through the middle, until it arrives at the end—you enter the third phase of writing. Now is the time to flesh out the ideas, to see if you have incorporated enough data or detail to make your argument muscular, your characters three-dimensional, your scenes real. Settling on the logic or the structure of the manuscript in the second phase creates the spine. During the third phase writers fatten their manuscript.

Next, we attend to the grace of expression. This is the moment to explore the use of the mot juste, the variety of sentence structure. To alternate short sentences with longer, more complex constructions, declarative sentences with conditional statements, questions with declarations. At this stage writers can sit with their writing and allow metaphors and similes to break the surface of their consciousness, flesh out important ideas with convincing details or supporting data, eliminate any redundancy, refine expression, trim away waste.

Only after seeing to the ideas, the logic, and the expression should you turn your attention to spelling, and after spelling to punctuation. These last two tasks amount to copyediting, and for some writers they are best left to experts. I was lucky. I took a course at the University of Iowa on sentence combining, and an unintended benefit of learning to create longer, more graceful sentences was an intuitive feel for where to place commas and semicolons. For many writers punctuation comes easily if they read their work aloud, noticing where they naturally pause in the telling. After all, grammar was created, not as an imposition on our language and our thinking, but as a vehicle to serve our thoughts and our expression. When we read what we have written out loud, we are able to listen to ourselves, to hear our own thinking. And as we read, we punctuate our thoughts naturally, organically, from within the workings of our own minds, and not from without, according to the dictates of grammarians.

That is what the process-approach toward writing is all about: giving ourselves as writers the time and space, the flexibility, and the permission to discover who we are on the page and what we want to say. It is about writing at our own pace, within personalized parameters, creating, as we move from the top of one page to the bottom of the next, a writing world that moves ahead with a speed and a rhythm that feel safe and appropriate for us. It is about preserving the peace.

Even writers who have chosen to devote two years to writing in a graduate program find it necessary to work at maintaining the truce. One of the students in an MFA workshop I am teaching wrote an essay about what he calls the most important discovery he's ever made about writing. This student has been writing for ten years, and for ten years he has struggled with the blank page. Like me he was a perpetual reviser, doubting his words as quickly as they landed on his computer screen, pressing the delete key hundreds of times as he worked his way through the first paragraph. This past summer, he told the workshop, he promised himself that he would complete at least two hundred pages of his major project, due at the end of the coming year. "Of course, the first day I sat down to write, I panicked completely. I must have been crazy to even think about writing so much." But a few minutes later he realized that to reach his goal he had to write only three pages a day. Maybe he could do that, he decided. And then something revolutionary happened. "I realized that I could write as much as I wanted if I didn't worry about how *good* the writing was." From that moment everything became possible for him. By shifting his focus from the writing itself, the product, to the experience of writing, or the process, this student unshackled himself from his anxiety about quality. Instead of writing at arm's length, poised always at the edge of the water, ready to judge what he wrote, he was able to dive into the experience of writing, to become one with the tap dance of his fingers on the keys, with the flow of words onto the page, one word after another, from the upper left-hand corner of the screen all the way to the bottom right.

As I write this book, I wonder what would happen if I still had to worry about misspellings at the same time that my mind roams to ferret out my ideas on writing and writing block. If, as I formed each sentence, I were simultaneously reformulating it for elegance. It is quite likely I would never discover how much I really know about my subject. Or what I think beyond my most accessible responses. Turning in so many directions at once, I would quickly become dizzy, able to focus upon and capture only what was closest at hand.

I have come to think of writing as a process in another larger way as well. When I became unblocked, for the first time I had a writing future. And for the first time I found myself feeling less pressured, less perfectionistic about whatever I was currently writing. If it wasn't stellar, perhaps what I wrote next would be. After all, I was improving all the time. All I had to do was look back to see how far I'd come. As I continued to write, I would continue to make discoveries. Not only would I take unanticipated side trips within each piece, but I might even find new and more pleasurable ways of traveling. Over the next few years my writing itself—my voice, style, even my purpose—might change. While I had once been a writing pessimist, I had become a writing optimist!

An attitude of optimism is particularly important for perfectionists. If you feel that every sentence you write must demonstrate intelligence and grace, if you view every memo or thank-you note as your last, you quickly become stuck. So much rides on every single word. Better to understand that, once you are unblocked, you will be able to write for the rest of your life. And if this particular example of your writing isn't Booker Prize material, perhaps something you write in the future may be!

I have seen this optimism spread to even the most stubborn of my clients. A lawyer I worked with was never able to reach closure on any of the chapters he wrote for his book. Each time we met and I suggested revisions, he would rewrite the chapter completely, from start to finish, so that, in place of a completed chapter, we had a new and radically different one. One day, instead of discussing the content of the chapter he brought for our meeting, I read the chapter aloud to him. When I finished, he said, "Hey, that was pretty good. Much better than I thought!"

As we talked, I realized that my client had never read over any of the chapters he had written before mailing them off to me. Instead, he wrote until the last minute, then slipped the pages into an envelope, never giving himself the opportunity to experience the chapter as a whole. What he was left with were all his stops and starts, the moments of struggle to articulate an idea or to figure out how best to present a concept. In his mind the chapter remained a jumble.

Hearing me read his writing, he was startled at the difference between his memory of what he wrote and what was actually on the page. Before we talked, this client had no sense of the process-approach to writing. He expected to create a finished product with the initial draft of each chapter. Because in his mind the pages he sent me were a jumbled mess, nothing at all like the polished and intelligent prose he hoped to create, they were not worth salvaging. Instead, each time he sat down to write, he felt obliged to begin all over again, in the hope that this time he would create the perfect text he imagined for his book.

Working together, we moved the chapter I read to him through the stages of revision, from first draft through logic and fleshing out to grace of prose, then to spelling and punctuation, until it was finally finished. "Now I see that I can, in fact, write," my client said. "I used to expect instant perfection. Now I understand that writing happens in stages. I may never be another Oliver Sacks, but I'll definitely be able to write more books. And I imagine my writing getting better with each one."

While the process-approach works well for most writers, it is not appropriate for everybody. Some writers do well with multitasking. I have watched a friend talk on the phone and knead pie dough or arrange a bouquet of flowers from her garden at the same time. Another friend invites guests for dinner and moves casually between the living room, where she socializes, and the kitchen, where she prepares the meal and plays with her dog. Both these women are exuberant writers and would squirm if forced to write within the confines of discrete stages. The more going on in their lives and on the page, the better.

I am not one of those people. I fall at the other extreme. I cannot even cook an omelette with full competence if someone is in the kitchen with me and I am trying to carry on a conversation. Perhaps it is because I am what someone once described as a kinesthetic responder. I react to stimuli with my whole body, all my senses zinging. For this reason I easily become overwhelmed and confused, and I need routine and order to get anything done. To me any disorder translates into chaos, while to my husband, Steve, a visual artist who responds to the world most strongly with his eyes, mess equals possibility. Abundance. Show him a pile of discarded wood, and he sees benches. A mound of stones tossed to the side of a trail and he thinks sculptures.

Although I came to understand that writing is a process, I am a perfectionist and so find it difficult to completely segregate the various stages of composing. While to overcome my block I strictly observed the successive-draft approach, proceeding faithfully from idea-generation to logic and fleshing-out, to polishing and on to copyediting, I no longer limit myself to idea-generation as the initial phase of my writing. If I delay revising too long, the instinct toward revision becomes unbearably strong. In the past, once this revision mania began, I was stuck, reviewing over and over again those first words, rearranging them, substituting alternatives, striking them, rearranging them yet a second and a third and fourth time until I was dizzy from the effort.

Now, within the new reign of peace, I do not allow disappointment and disapproval to saturate my writing experience. I neither judge my prose as I compose, nor condemn my perfectionism. Instead of fighting against myself, I accept my desire for perfection at the same time that I work to modulate it. I acknowledge that I am unable to simply sit down and write freely, concentrating uniquely on generating ideas. Afraid of becoming lost in a warren of words and sentences that lead nowhere, I do not try to force myself to surrender fully to the blank page. I still revise as I write, but I have taught myself patience, delaying revision for greater and greater increments of time.

Once you are no longer at war with yourself as a writer, you will find it easier to turn off the switch that leads you to delete and type, delete and type, delete and type, word by word by word. By reminding yourself that this is only the first draft, or the second, you will be able to move through the revision more quickly than ever before. You will no longer feel every word and phrase is a life-or-death matter. And you will develop strategies to help *keep* you writing once you begin, ways of approaching even the first draft that honor your perfectionism and at the same time prevent you from becoming blocked.

I arrived at this process progressively. Initially I made a mental contract with myself that I would not look back at what I had written until I had completed the first paragraph. At the time even this limitation was a stretch for me. While my rational self wanted to set the limit at one full typed page before I began revising, my anxious self was frightened of promising to delay for even one paragraph. It helped to remind myself that this was not a permanent arrangement, that my writing parameters could evolve as I became more comfortable with the process. Now I am not tempted to look back until the first few pages are written, and

I expect that in the future I will draft for a longer time before the revision bug bites. This doesn't mean that all my anxiety magically dissipated. Knowing that at first I had to write without looking back for what to me seemed like forever did indeed cause a charge of fear to shoot through me. But for the first time the charge didn't swell to full-blown panic. I knew that after one full paragraph I could begin to improve what was on the page. I had also learned that a modicum of discomfort is not fatal to my writing process.

This is important to overcoming writing block: realizing that we can still write, even if we don't feel 100 percent relaxed. I'm not implying that you should attempt writing when you feel panic or extreme discomfort. Certainly not. Forcing yourself to write under these conditions intensifies negative associations with writing and can strengthen the block. No, what I am suggesting is that, even if you don't feel completely in the mood or inspired, even if you feel a twinge of discomfort, you should still sit down and try to write. For five, ten, or fifteen minutes. You might well discover that, as you write, the panic that nipped at your heels at the beginning of the session gradually dissipates. Or that your mood shifts and you begin to relax into the process. What matters here is that you not expect always to feel joyous at the prospect of writing or during those first moments in front of the blank page.

Most experienced writers admit to periodic bouts of anxiety or depression. Some confront these states more frequently and more intensely than others. It is not these feelings themselves that interfere with our ability to write, but our response to these feelings. If we panic and tell ourselves, "I'm too nervous to write today; I'll go shopping instead," or, "If I'm this nervous, my writing will never be any good," and we avoid writing, we feed our own insecurities, helping them grow stronger and bolder and lengthening the distance between our desire to write and our ability to do so. If, instead, we tell ourselves, "I'm nervous about writing today, but I'll give it a try," we narrow the gap between *writing* and *not writing,* between our desire to write and our ability to do so.

I discovered that, if I honored the terms of my truce, I could work through my initial uneasiness and write my way to a more relaxed state. One of the important factors for me in creating this momentum was my series of temporary contracts with myself about how long I would write before I looked back. Over time I was able to lengthen the amount of my initial writing, first to two paragraphs and then on to three and four, one full page and then two. But I made these changes slowly, only after I had experienced an extended period of comfort at my current level.

Many blocked writers find provisional contracts helpful. At first some do best by limiting output to a single paragraph or two. For others a set period of time works well. I once had a client who had been blocked for many years and had accumulated such a sea of anxiety around writing that even the thought of a single sentence sent her blood pressure on the rise. After we had worked together to help her sit down and consider the possibility of writing, we decided that her safety limit was no longer than sixty seconds. So she began, alternating one minute of writing with one minute of rest. At first she was dubious about this arrangement. "How will I ever be able to write a full short story when I'm forced to hobble like this?" she asked.

"You'll see," was all I could respond. "You'll see."

And she did see; ever so slowly, but visibly, she was able to increase her writing increments, from one to two minutes, from two to five, and so on. Seeing such improvement after years of struggle and anguish helped renew this writer's faith in herself, another important factor in overcoming block. And once her faith began to return, it fueled her improvement, so that the increments became longer and longer until she was well on her way to considering herself a writer again.

The peace process is never formulaic. It takes into account the cultures and personalities of the countries that have previously been at war. Writers can personalize the strategies they put into place to maintain peace in their writing world. By becoming aware of their writing process and observing themselves during the various stages of composing, they can begin to notice what situations and conditions are most favorable to their success.

If, for instance, you have the most energy and optimism in the morning, it makes sense to schedule writing time within the first few hours of the day. Conversely, if you feel calmer and more receptive in the evening, when the day no longer holds surprises, it might be best to think about writing once you have finished dinner and cleaned up the kitchen. Some of us feel safest in the full light of day, while others can only relax once the sun begins to set. Honoring these natural rhythms and perceptions, the ways and the times we work best, is essential if our writing experience is to be positive.

Sustaining peace is a process of collaboration, not imposition. A collaboration of writers with themselves. No one strategy works for everyone. As writers we need to feel our way through the process, observing, sensing, acknowledging when and how we feel most comfortable working, and then implement what we discover about our preferences. The collaboration begins with our noticing how we live our lives in general. With paying attention to when we feel most relaxed. Happiest. At peace. And with noticing the ways we encourage ourselves at difficult or challenging moments. If you run marathons, how do you take the first steps, knowing you have twenty-six miles ahead of you? And when you've run thirteen of those miles, with thirteen more to go, how do you keep yourself from feeling discouraged? Or if you plan a large dinner party, how do you keep from feeling overwhelmed? How is it that you don't think immediately of all the cleaning up you will be left with after the guests have gone home? Or of all the possible failures in a meal that begins with appetizers and concludes with dessert? Whatever you tell yourself to keep running or cooking may be transferable to writing. To motivate yourself to write, you can use whatever tactics you employ to get out of bed every morning and run or to don your chef's hat and begin the preparations for a meal you have spent hours planning.

One of my clients, a professional in the business world, was an amateur musician, and loved playing Bach sonatas on her violin. Her bow flying, body swaying with the music, life felt fluid, harmonious, the notes, the measures, the left and right hands working together to create a whole that was pleasing to the ear. This was starkly different from the state she entered when she tried to write. There, fluency was denied her; her words seemed to clash, to sputter and fail.

I suggested that she play the violin for fifteen minutes or so before she sat down to write. Perhaps the world of her writing would no longer seem inimical if associated with her world of music. Perhaps the harmony of the music would accompany her to her computer. This strategy worked for several weeks, during which my client tapped into a fluency with her writing she had never experienced before. But then the association stopped working, and fifteen minutes into her writing the world again turned

into a cacophony. "I could hear bells clanging and birds screech-
ing as I tried to write," she told me. "It was awful. I wanted to
cover my ears."

"What if you tape your music and play the tape while you
write?" I suggested. "Maybe the part of you that is so fluent with
the violin will lend itself to you as writer."

And this is what happened. By taping herself playing the violin and by playing this tape while she wrote, my client brought
the musician part of herself with her into the writing room, right
to the computer screen. While she wrote, measures of Bach
floated toward her, filling the air with a harmony and a fluency
the writer herself had produced. Gradually the keyboard of her
computer became the strings of her violin, and the fluidity she
experienced while playing Bach began to characterize her writing. She noticed that she held her hands differently as she wrote.
That her posture had changed, her back and neck now straighter,
as if she were standing with her violin, not sitting on her chair.
She even found herself swaying to her words, as if the letters had
become notes.

It isn't hard to negotiate the truce agreement and maintain a
lasting peace in your writing world. The peace process only asks
that you pay attention to what you love, your passion, to what
makes you laugh or chuckle. To when you feel best about yourself. Once you understand the situations and circumstances that
allow you to display your feathers, you can figure out how to
bring these circumstances to your writing experience.

Since writing is about your relationship with yourself, you
have the right—indeed the obligation—to shape this relationship
so that it is perfectly suited to you. Thinking you should write the
way anybody else writes is as misguided as thinking your personality should mimic someone else's. Once you realize this, once

you realize that you have everything you need within yourself to write, you will become your own best security, and you will, at last, be able to take off that bullet-proof vest and slip into the shirt you feel most comfortable wearing.

Try This

1. Make a diagram of the stages a manuscript passes through from beginning to completion: first draft = sowing of ideas; second draft = harvesting and organizing ideas according to your logic; third draft = fertilizing ideas with additional details or data; fourth draft = surveying the prose for style and grace; fifth draft = weeding out misspelling and poor punctuation. Remind yourself that you are only responsible for one task with each draft, and anytime you start to think ahead, bring yourself back to the task at hand.

2. Precede your writing time with an activity that infuses you with a feeling of competence. If you enjoy playing the piano or doing yoga, singing or whipping up something in the kitchen, set aside fifteen minutes to a half hour for this activity before you intend to write. Remind yourself as you begin that you feel competent and effective and that you can feel the same way while writing.

3. When you finish writing each day jot down any positive writing experiences or moments you have had. Every few days read through your entries, allowing yourself to absorb and reexperience the good feelings writing is beginning to evoke.

4. If you are beginning to feel more comfortable writing, you might create a long-term contract with yourself. Remembering not to think too large, envision your writing goals for the next few months, starting slowly and only gradually

increasing either your writing time or your anticipated output. It's usually best to remain at each interval for at least two weeks. The goal of the contract is to encourage, not to push, yourself.

11

Becoming Your Own Best Friend

When one of my newest clients began working with me several months ago, she was thrilled at how much easier it was to write when she knew somebody was going to read what she put on the page. For a month or two she was able to find the time to sit down on a regular basis, and before each of our meetings I received a nearly completed story. Then one week she apologized because all she had managed to write was a revision of a piece we had looked at together several meetings earlier. "I think I've been too busy socially these past two weeks to get enough writing time in," she explained. "I went out to dinner twice, and I had a group of friends over for a movie marathon this weekend. After all that interaction it was hard to clear my head enough to write."

The following meeting, two weeks later, she brought a partial revision of another piece. "It must be work that's keeping me from setting aside time to write. My assistant left several months ago, and I'm having to take up all the slack."

Two weeks later she called to ask if we could postpone our scheduled meeting. "Too much has been happening lately for me to see my way to writing. Work is hectic. I'm getting ready for a trip to China. A friend from out of town visited last weekend," she explained. "I just haven't had any time. Could we reschedule?"

Instead of postponing the meeting, I asked if she would come and talk. I told her that it wasn't unusual for the writers I work with to hit a wall after the first few sessions, and that it might help to discuss what was happening.

When my client walked into my office a few days later, she smiled as she handed me a new story. "I've been reading a book on relationships, and I realized that writing is not all that different from my relationship with Tom. It's easy at the beginning. Commitment is what causes all the problems. I figured my problem was that I wasn't committed enough to my writing. 'If you want to write,' I told myself, 'you'd better buckle down!' "

This writer had indeed made an important discovery. "You're right," I said. "Writing is all about relationship. In fact, I've discovered that for me it's the most important relationship in my life."

"More important than your relationship with Steve?" she asked.

Yes, I nodded, realizing I'd never told this to anyone before, never said aloud that writing was more important than anything else in my life. More important than my husband. More important than my son. Which doesn't mean that I could live happily without them. That my life wouldn't feel desolate if they were not a part of it. No. Stating that writing is my most important relationship means that writing lies at the heart of my life. It is what sends the blood coursing through everything else that I do. If my writing isn't going well, my life becomes anemic, and everything else pales—my passion for teaching, for Steve, for Jonah, for my garden, for my friends. I pass my days in a fog, fuzzy headed, disoriented, unable to focus, to pay attention even to what is right in front of me.

I'm not talking here about an unhappy hour or two, or even a few days. What I mean by my writing not going well is a longer period of time, a week or more of not sitting down to write because I am too busy with work or with complications in my life. What I mean by my writing not going well is over and over again feeling unhappy with what I have written. By my writing not going well, I mean much more than one or two downward blips on the radar screen.

If writing lies at the very center of my life, I have to expect it to be alive, to pulse, to course, to pant, to sigh, to surge, and at moments even to pause. In fact, one of the ways I have learned not to panic when I write is to understand—and accept—that my writing life will exhibit the same level of variability, the same pattern of ups and downs, of excess and near-deprivation, as the rest of my life.

Think about it. Writing is a relationship, and in any relationship we can't expect to feel blissful day in and day out. There are too many variables, too many other people and circumstances that interfere. I have too many bills to pay. Too many errands to run. I lose a filling, forget to move the car on street-cleaning day and receive a ticket. I'm late to meet Steve for dinner. Steve's back hurts. We are prickly. Irritable. Distracted. We bicker. He tells me I'm yelling. I complain about his mess. He complains about my complaining. We argue. I head out back for my office. He sits down with a book. And we stay that way, in our separate spheres, huffing and puffing, until we remember how much we love each other and meet up again to embrace.

Some days you may bicker with your writing. Some days you may not see eye to eye. You write a paragraph, decide it's flat, and erase it. You tell a story, realize it's not relevant, and press the delete key. Or, reading over what you've written, you see that you are writing in circles, saying the same thing again and again, not making headway. Or you read and realize your words are stale. Your prose too thin. Too ornate. Too dense. All these annoyances, these setbacks, these moments of malaise—you have to expect them. And to keep writing.

When Steve and I have a turbulent day, I don't think our partnership is bad. I understand: We are temporarily navigating rough seas. In the same way, I don't hear alarms go off after several sessions of stuttering on the page. I have learned patience with my writing, learned tolerance for myself and the vicissitudes of my writing life. I no longer see each hesitation as a sign of danger, each slow day as prelude to silence.

My client was right. Writing is a relationship, a give-and-take between the writer and the activity of putting words down on the page. This is an intimate relationship, one that asks for the cooperation of all our possible selves. To write we need to rally all that we are—the permissive parent, the good friend, the artist, the thinker, the child within each of us—and ask them to collaborate, to work together to help us to sit down and translate into words what is best in ourselves—our playfulness, our profundity, our wisdom, our inspiration.

Understanding that writing involves relationship provides a template for the best ways to treat ourselves when we want to write. If you accept that you should treat your writing the way you treat a partner, you begin to realize that commanding yourself to sit down and write might not be the best way to achieve results. It still surprises me that, when people have trouble writing, they view themselves as enemies, declare martial law, send in the troops. Suddenly they would use force against themselves, make unilateral declarations, take away their own freedom. One of my clients ordered himself home each evening by seven o'clock, seven nights a week—until he finished his dissertation. Another client told me, "I was so angry at myself for not writing that I punished myself by staying away from my garden all week."

If you felt that your partner was avoiding you, would you order that she stay home at night or spend night after night talking? When you heard the key turn in the door at midnight, would you curse and scream? Would you demand that she not see any of her friends again until you felt more secure in your relationship? That she spend every free waking hour with you? Would you make her feel guilty, tell her she was ruining your life?

Of course, we've all tried these approaches at some time in our lives. And we've all learned the same lesson: They don't work. With enough reflection, enough counseling, enough discussion—enough failure—we discover that hostility and commandeering usually produce the opposite result. Our partner avoids us even more. Our conversations become increasingly formulaic. We sense our abandonment more keenly.

For all parties in a relationship to flourish, they must feel safe, physically and emotionally. Acts of force and aggression are received as attacks. Of you against your partner. Or, in the case of writing, of one part of you against another. Immediately the remaining parts mobilize for our defense. And defense involves moving away from, not moving toward. *Don't you dare threaten me like that. I don't want to write anyway. I have better things to do. Exercise is more important. I deserve a break. Who do you think you are? Try and make me. Try and catch me. Poor me, why is everything so difficult? I never liked you anyway. Who needs you?*

One of the best ways to promote safety in any relationship is to ban absolute mandates. No more pushing yourself around. Ordering yourself to write. Or to stay in the house if you are not writing. Or to produce a certain number of pages or words per day. For my new client, this meant rescinding her order to "just sit down and write" and setting up a more reasonable schedule.

"Okay, I won't demand as much from myself, but from now on I'll stay home every night so that I won't be too tired to write in the morning," she suggested.

"That still sounds a little commandeering to me," I responded. "Let's modify that a bit. How about deciding to stay home two nights a week so that you can write two mornings a week?"

"That sounds fine," she said. "I'll get up at five o'clock and write until seven."

"Slow down," I said. "At the beginning I would suggest getting up at six-thirty and writing until seven."

"That's not enough time to get anything done," she worried.

"What's most important is that you experience consistent, unpressured time to write," I told her. "And, you'll see, a half hour is plenty of time for your writing to accumulate into a finished piece. Just keep reminding yourself that you're doing the right thing," I urged.

Writing involves partnership with yourself, and an important component of partnership is dialogue and conversation. As writers we have to learn to speak and then to listen to what we have to say. How often we complain about our partners not really heeding what we tell them! And yet I've discovered how hard it is for the writers I work with to listen—I mean really listen—to themselves.

"I've learned to talk to myself lately, and that's helped my writing fluidity a lot," one of my students mentioned in class last night. "Whenever I feel panic, I remind myself to be kind. It all started with my asking myself, 'What would you tell your girl-friend if she were feeling this way?' And then one day I realized that, if I wanted to be able to write, I had to become my own best friend."

"Exactly," I said. For, some time ago, I too had discovered that if I wanted to continue writing, free of block, I had to treat myself like my own best friend. And although I don't remember the precise moment I made this discovery, like my student I remember what I was thinking at the time. And I remember the experience of listening deeply to what I had to say—so deeply that I could feel the words sinking into my skin like a fine mist. Stuck, I had launched into my usual stream of self-criticism when I became aware of the cruelty I was inflicting on myself. *You would never speak this way to your friends,* I thought. And then an idea occurred to me—an idea that now seems obvious but at the time was as fantastic for me as the possibility of life on Mars. *Why don't you try talking to yourself as if you were your own friend?*

And I was launched. Like my student, I had taken my first step into a new world—a world of possibilities where I would dis-cover a completely new repertory of responses to my own dis-tress. Instead of punishing myself I could encourage myself, be understanding, compassionate, empathic. Instead of comman-deering myself I could collaborate, converse with myself to dis-cover the best ways to keep writing. I could become my own coach, my fellow team member. "That's the way; you're doing a good job," I could say. "Of course you're nervous; the blank page makes all writers anxious." "Don't worry if your writing isn't going well today. It went well yesterday. And it may go well tomorrow." "You can always revise, so don't panic about what you've just written."

Since that day, when I planted the very first seed of self-compassion, I have watched a forest grow up around me. From that single, "That's the way, Jane Anne," so many varieties of trees now surround me, some forming dense thickets, others the laciest of screens. "Don't worry, Jane Anne, you always manage to finish. I know it's slow today, but remember how quickly you wrote last week. Even if you write only one paragraph a day, you will be able to finish this essay by the end of the month." "This might not be one of your best essays, chapters, or stories, but you'll write many more."

Each of us has to discover how to become our own best friend as we write. In my personal life I have friends who tell me their troubles and want my advice. If I only listened, without responding and advising, they would feel abandoned. But I have other friends who need my presence, not my words. With me they hope to find the peace and safety to think through a problem out loud. I help them most by witnessing and supporting, not by advising.

When these friends and I first met, we didn't know any of this about each other. It took time. It took being together and watching, considering what seemed to help us through difficulty and what seemed to interfere. In the same way, writers don't know exactly how to best behave toward themselves when they start writing. That is why it is so important to be aware of the way the writing process works for you.

One of the most important questions writers can ask themselves is, "What kind of friend would I want to spend time with?" Do you gravitate toward people who are overtly supportive, offering frequent and profuse compliments, or do you feel more comfortable with a quieter, more implicit brand of support, more like a quick nod of the head or meeting of the eyes in approval? Do you prefer strong disagreement or oblique questions? Criticism or suggestion? The answers are not easy. Each of us warms to different modes of interaction and response. I prefer clear reactions. If Steve doesn't like the way I am driving, I want him to tell me, sweetly, what I am doing that makes him uncomfortable. Am I passing too slowly, weaving within my own lane? Since I am a perfectionist, if there's any way to improve my performance, I'm enthusiastic. In addition, if I sense Steve's discomfort and have to worry about its source, I can hardly pay attention to the road.

Steve is just the opposite. He hears suggestions as criticism. I say, "Isn't the speed limit seventy-five miles per hour?" and he's certain I'm thoroughly impugning his driving—everything from the play of his foot on the clutch to his attitude toward other drivers. With him I've had to learn to curb my reactivity, commenting only when my observation seems essential.

Anyone who has ever been in a relationship knows how much work is involved in tuning ourselves to our partner while at the same time making certain not to tune ourselves out. How much easier it should be if we are going solo, responsible only for ourselves. And yet the writers I work with often don't know how to treat themselves. Even after we have talked together about writing as a relationship, they have no idea how to embrace themselves and the kinds of writers they are and will continue to become.

To sustain a productive relationship with our writing, we have to learn new behaviors toward ourselves, new ways of responding *to,* instead of reacting *against,* the way we write. At first this involves altering expectations and setting modest goals, always working within parameters that feel comfortable to us. Once we have discovered how to support ourselves in these ways, we are ready to learn how to reinforce and nourish the relationship. In other words, we don't grow as writers simply by learning to avoid self-criticism. We progress by giving ourselves permission to write and supporting ourselves in the process. This means we must learn how to reward ourselves for doing what we said we wanted to do: sitting down on a regular basis and writing.

Think about what it's like both to have and to be a best friend. First, the relationship implies intimacy. As we mature, we establish closeness with our friends through conversation and support about what matters most to us—work, family, other friends, romance. When it's working, this kind of friendship is a true collaboration, each party present for the other in multiple ways. We talk, we listen, we suggest, we agree, we question, we differ. And we learn, through exposure, when to enact each of these behaviors.

This is what my client who commanded herself to be more committed to her writing needed to understand. What was important was that she spend her time writing in a manner that felt comfortable to her, that she treat herself with kindness and understanding. The way she had talked when she first arrived for our meeting, she sounded like an officer commanding a platoon of new recruits. "Instead of putting yourself in boot camp," I suggested, "why not imagine yourself at a spa each morning? Or at a retreat. Gentle yourself into writing. Tell yourself, 'I know it's hard for you to sit down and write, but you did it last week and managed to create a few darned good pages.' Or, 'It's okay if you feel a little nervous, you'll feel better soon.' Or, 'I know just how you feel. But I've also heard you talking about what you are writing with a lot of pride.'"

It's difficult, if not impossible, to prescribe the conversations writers should have within themselves. This is not the universe of aphorisms and adages. It is the territory of relationships and intimacy, and to understand you have to be situated right smack in the middle. In the same way that we learn about our friends and friendships gradually, bit by bit over time, writers establish partnerships with themselves around their writing slowly, through trial and error, through intuition and not logic. It is up to each writer to discover the particular give-and-take necessary to support the relationship.

You may be surprised by what you learn about yourself. After all, it is rare that we are in a position to receive precisely what we need. Most often the back-and-forth between friends involves compromise, whether conscious or not. Coming together as friends involves giving up some territories while claiming others. If one of my friends is a militant vegetarian, I might well decide not to mention the delicious roast suckling pig I was served at a dinner party. Likewise, knowing that I am soft on dogs, she may refrain from mentioning a grizzly scene she witnessed in the park between an owner and his runaway puppy. After a while we do not make these decisions consciously. Instead, our relationship to one another has become internalized, and a great deal of the way we behave has become natural and inevitable.

A few years ago, when I began writing my book on walking around the track, I decided to set aside the time from 8:00 until 11:00 A.M. each day for walking and writing. Which I did. I slid out of bed every morning, walked the three blocks down to the track, and was at my computer no later than 9:30. I did all this before cleaning up the kitchen, listening to my answering machine, making my bed. One day, about three months into the routine, I became aware of a voice in my head. Not the sound of the previous chorus, the cacophony of criticism and abuse I had once worked so hard to tune out. No, it was a new voice, sweet and soft, and it was saying, *You're a good girl. You're doing just what you set out to do. You're a good girl.*

At first I was incredulous. Who was inside my head, speaking such kindness to me? Quickly I felt annoyed and embarrassed. The voice was infantilizing me, talking to me as if I were a little girl. How ridiculous! I tried to stop listening. But the voice remained, sweet and insistent: *You're a good girl, a good girl.*

The next morning at the track, I thought back to my experience of the day before and began to understand. I had entered a new phase in my relationship with my writing. Until then, although I had considered myself a writer, I had thought of myself equally as a teacher, a mother, a partner, a friend, a daughter, and a gardener. All this had begun to shift once I committed myself to walking and writing every morning for a year. The commitment had surfaced naturally, from within, one day as I was walking casually around the track. It was not imposed by my thinking mind, from arm's length, out of a sense of obligation. Immediately my plan felt right. And over the few months during which I had honored this commitment, my mornings felt more and more congruent with my life and the direction in which I was headed. The voice, then, was simply affirming the goodness of something new and appropriate. This new relationship with myself and my writing was still in its infancy. Who knew where it would take me, what it would develop into? But for now the cronish, arthritic voices in my head had been replaced by a new voice, and for the moment this new voice understood that what I was doing was right and good.

Try This

1. Think of your relationships with your close friends and write a profile of yourself as a friend, isolating those qualities that show what you bring to the relationship. Once you have isolated these qualities, think about how you enact them when your friends need you.

2. Now think about your writing and reflect upon how you can bring your best qualities into this relationship. Imagine how you can respond to yourself—as if you were your own friend—when you are feeling discouraged or overwhelmed or stuck or anxious. Imagine what overtures or interventions of friendship you can make to encourage your writing.

3. If you encounter a dry spell with your writing, or feel that it is on the skids, invite yourself to sit down and have a heart-to-heart talk. During this conversation, refrain from accusation and criticism and consider instead how best to help yourself. Begin by reviewing what you have discovered about your relationship with writing and determine whether you have been ignoring anything you have learned. As you reflect, think about any ways in which you have failed to respect yourself in the past weeks or months. Decide how to remedy the negative dynamic. Remind yourself, again and again if necessary, that you are your ally, your own best friend.

12

What Do You Want to Write?

One of my clients had been writing short fiction, with some success. She had been a resident at a writing retreat several times. Her work had even been noticed by one of the notable writers at the retreat. And she had published a few stories in literary magazines. Yet, at a certain point in her writing career, shortly after receiving her master's degree in creative writing, my client was no longer able to write stories. Not a word. Despite this block she easily polished off the grant proposals she was responsible for writing at work. In fact, she was often praised for the proposals, both by her coworkers and the grant readers in Washington, D.C. But the good feelings did not transfer to her fiction writing. So she made an appointment to see me.

"I know I have some talent. Other writers have told this to me. And I know I want to write. In fact, I want more of my life to revolve around writing. So what's my problem? Why, when I sit down to begin a story, do I feel completely dried up? Unable to think of anything to say?"

I hadn't had time to get to know my client well enough to answer her questions or even to speculate about her situation. But from what she told me, I understood that her current inability to write had its source someplace deep within her. For this writer many of the components of a successful writing life seemed to be in place. Because she had only recently experienced her block, I didn't think she was writing for the wrong audience—hers had at one time offered high praise for her writing. I guessed that she had learned to behave kindly toward herself when she wrote, since she was able to complete writing projects of a different genre. And if she completed grant proposals easily, the voices in her head couldn't be entirely negative. What then did she need to shift in order to engage the creative part of herself once again?

For many weeks we talked. I suggested strategies to prime her fiction pump. This client liked to paint, so I asked her to try writing stories about her paintings. I also suggested that she limit her writing time. More specifically, I asked her to sit down in front of her computer only a half hour before she was due to leave the house for work. I also mentioned writing about only one color or one image from the painting she was currently working on. I didn't want the prospect of writing about an entire canvas to overwhelm her. Most important, I discussed with my client rewarding herself each time she successfully wrote for a half hour.

"How can I do that?" she asked.

"Listen to your favorite track on your favorite CD. Read a chapter in a good book. Meditate. Call your best friend. Take your dog for a walk. Engage in any activity you look forward to," I answered.

My client tried all these tactics. She chose a painting to write about. She sat down to write at 12:15 each day, exactly forty-five minutes before she had to leave for work. She wrote about the color blue. And when she stopped writing at 12:45, she relaxed on the couch, listening to Joan Armatrading or Bonnie Raitt for fifteen minutes. But after several months she had written only a few isolated paragraphs. And she had become increasingly upset. "I've always dreamed of writing. But it looks like I'm going to have to give up on my dream," she told me one day. "It's time that I accepted the fact that I can't write."

"Do you really want to accept not writing as a permanent state?" I asked.

"Of course not!" she was quick to reply. "The minute those words are out of my mouth, I can't imagine what my life would be like without writing. Writing is what has always helped me move toward the future—the dream that one day I'd spend a part of each day crafting stories."

"You know," I responded, "maybe you've been trying to write the wrong stories. I've noticed how much pleasure you get telling family tales—about your childhood, about your parents and your brother, about your grandparents and your aunts and uncles. I wonder what would happen if you shifted genres and tried nonfiction."

She looked at me with surprise, then shrugged. "It's worth a try," she said. "I'm desperate."

This conversation took place on a Friday. The following week my client walked into my office and handed me a twenty-page manuscript. "You were right," she said, smiling.

After she had left my office the previous week, my client had gone straight home, booted up her computer, and begun writing the story of her disastrous first swimming lessons, when she had nearly drowned. That first afternoon she had worked for two hours straight, until she and her husband had to get ready to go to dinner with friends. The following week she got up an hour early every morning and wrote before leaving for work. As the days passed and her manuscript grew, she became more and more elated.

"Did you think it would be this easy?" she asked after I had looked through the pages I held in my hands. "Did you ever imagine I would bring in a completed story this week?"

Of course I hadn't. While I was quite hopeful that the shift in genre would help her, I did not know how far this modification would carry my client. It might only take her through the gate or across the moat, where she might well encounter additional threats. There was no way for me to know or predict what other obstacles to her writing might arise. This time we were both lucky; transferring from fiction to nonfiction was all it took.

Later, while discussing this rapid transformation, my client suggested that what had helped her write so easily in nonfiction was the familiarity and safety of her stories. "Sure, I didn't know everything I would eventually write. But at least I knew all the characters pretty well. And I knew how things were going to turn out, even if my life at the time I was writing about was disastrous."

Writing fiction, she had felt just the opposite. Her fiction had emerged nearly unbidden, mysteriously, uncontrollably. One day she might be in line at the supermarket, and a character would present himself to her. Another time she might be walking her dog, and an image would appear. Or a story unfold out of whole cloth in her head. This process, while thrilling at times, left my client feeling out of control and powerless. Not only did she never know when fiction might offer itself to her, she didn't know from minute to minute what she would write. "It was as if I were channeling," she told me. "I almost had to push my conscious mind out of the way." While some writers relish this state of transport, it had begun to make my client uneasy. "I never knew what was going to appear on the page, and perhaps I'm just too old for all that suspense!" Writing nonfiction, she felt more powerful, more knowing, and these attributes seemed more appropriate for the person she felt she wanted—and needed—to be. "Never knowing from day to day what I was going to write, what was going to appear on the page, made me feel helpless. I was never on sure footing, and this began to make me more and more anxious."

Of course, when we sit down to write, we cannot—and should not—know exactly what we will inscribe on the page. In fact, many writers describe writing as a process of discovery, a journey of happening upon and unearthing what it is we are writing about. And indeed, for many writers, the exploration of a story or a topic of interest—even of the contents of a letter—is part of what attracts and engages them in writing.

The degree of mystery, the balance of certainty and discovery, we can embrace comfortably varies from writer to writer, and from time to time in the course of our lives. Some writers may begin, fresh out of school, as journalists, at ease with facts only. Then, feeling more and more confident as writers over the course of a career as reporters, they begin to feel constrained by the facts and want to branch out into editorials and personal essays. While other writers, proud of an active imagination, with a desire to take risks, may begin by writing fiction, insisting on "inventing the facts of the story," until one day life itself offers up a real story too delicious to resist. Still other writers, who feel uncomfortable with the story of their life, find they must embrace fiction to continue to write.

A writer I work with took this path from nonfiction to fiction. Although he could begin pieces fluidly, he had trouble with endings. Always, no matter how well he had launched the piece, he began to stumble just when it was time to create closure. So he would begin another story, planning to return to the previous piece in a week or two. By the time we began working together, he had at least fifteen unfinished manuscripts piled on his desk.

Like many nonfiction writers this man was writing about his family. When he had first begun, the picture he thought he was about to draw was one of privilege and idiosyncrasy, glamour and brilliance. But the more he wrote the less the pictures he produced matched those he had anticipated. His camera seemed to have a mind of its own. While he thought he was snapping one scene, it focused on another. Or, while he wanted to concentrate on the foreground, the camera penetrated deeper. The images appearing were painful to him—images of a father who was jealous of his wife and their three handsome sons, of a mother whose chief characteristic was vanity. This was far from the conscious vision my client held of his family as a close-knit unit whose lives had been filled with culture and adventure. It began to make sense that he had difficulty bringing any of his pieces to closure. As long as they were unfinished, the endings uncertain, the plots tentative, he didn't have to confront the unhappy realities of his childhood. Incomplete, his stories could always change.

It took me a while to understand this. To see that my client was blocked by the reality of his childhood. At first I was swept along by the veneer of his parents' prosperity and intelligence. By the refinement and subtlety of my client's prose. It took several months of conversation and failed unblocking strategies to grasp what was at stake for him. Once I did, I asked if he had ever considered writing fiction.

"That seems like a cop-out," he replied. "I'm stuck, so instead of finding my way through the impasse, you're suggesting I switch my destination. Or my mode of transportation?"

"Perhaps only temporarily," I told him. "Being stuck for too long has negative side effects. Writers who assume that they should tough it out often make things worse for themselves, creating permanent damage. It's better to write than not to write, and at a certain point my goal in working with you is to find a way—any way—to keep you writing."

"You mean writing fiction might unblock me, and once I'm unblocked, I can return to nonfiction?"

"Exactly. What's important now is to stop your downward spiral, to prevent you from continuing to accumulate negative experiences that only reinforce your negative feelings about writing. Once you accumulate enough positive responses in your writing account, we can talk about returning to nonfiction."

Within a year my client moved to the East Coast and entered an MFA program in fiction writing. The last I heard from him, he was experiencing no difficulty completing the short stories he inaugurated. Many, but not all, of his characters were based on his parents, and his plots were often drawn from his childhood. However, now he was in charge of the personalities of his protagonists and antagonists, of what happened when. If the main character in one story was arrogant or narcissistic or vain, he could soften any of these traits by imbuing him with true grace, a warm wit, a tragic flaw. If the ending of the real story was too painful, he could invent another, sunnier one. Or he could eliminate the darkest moments from a narrative. For him fiction writing was much like painting on a black-and-white photograph. If the subject's face is too dark, the artist can lighten it with a touch of yellow. If the background is too chaotic, that can be rectified by applying a unifying tint.

There is no one genre, no single subject, no particular voice a writer is meant to engage. Writing is about self-expression, about depicting the world within your heart, your memory, your mind. To depict this world, a writer needs to feel safe. Shifting genres may provide this profound safety.

To help secure this necessary asylum, blocked writers can

compose their short stories, their business memos, or their legal briefs in the form of letters to friends. To diminish their fear of the finality of the written word, others might try speaking their narratives into a tape recorder. Journalists who suddenly find that they are unable to produce their usual pieces can try shifting from feature writing to more-traditional news writing. Blocked news writers might also explore creative nonfiction narrative. And Ph.D. candidates who cannot finish their dissertations can explore strategies for personalizing their academic writing so that it feels more familiar to them—less like a document they are writing for a lofty and learned audience and more like a manuscript they are producing for their own pleasure. For some of these writers safety involves shifting away from the strictly academic by incorporating descriptive or process-oriented prose into their academic writing. For others it involves navigating from the impersonal prose of the traditional dissertation to a more personal style by incorporating the narrator's presence within the text.

One of my newest clients came to me after a productive academic career. He had recently retired and thought he would use his newfound time to write additional articles in his field. But he discovered that, for the first time in his life, he was unable to write. "I have a bibliography of over fifty articles, and I never had a minute of difficulty writing any one of them. And now, when I finally have time to write even more, the well seems to have run dry."

As we began to work together, I noticed that my client often began our sessions by telling me stories about his graduate career and the serendipitous events that led him to his field of study, so one day I suggested that he might enjoy writing about one of the twists or turns in his career. "That might be fun," he responded.

"I already have all the material. It shouldn't be too difficult to write it up."

Two weeks later he almost skipped into my office. "Who would have ever guessed that I, the inveterate scientist, would have so much fun writing about my own life!"

Since then he has continued to write about his career, and he hasn't yet mentioned his vast bibliography of academic articles. I imagine that he will finish telling his story, and then perhaps he will return to writing the scientific articles he intended to write when he first came to see me. For now, however, he is no longer blocked, and I am quite sure that the change in his status from active researcher and professor to retiree demanded a change in the kind of writing he engaged in, at least for a while.

My writing autobiography includes successive genre shifts, as I discovered more and more deeply how to make writing safe. I began as a poet. Then after teaching freshman English for several years, moved to nonfiction prose. In those days I wrote about other people. People I interviewed. People I observed in small scenes of everyday life. People who entertained me with their stories. Whenever anyone suggested I write about myself, I retorted, "Oh, that's not the kind of writing I do. Other people are more interesting to me."

In hindsight, I think I believed that I had to keep myself out of my writing if I wanted to remain unstuck. In order to have access to words and expression on the page, I needed to turn my back on my own experiences, remain at a safe distance from my own stories. During my year of walking around the track, I began writing short pieces about my experience, and the more I wrote, the more familiar the person on the page sounded to me. The more I recognized her personality. Her way of thinking. Of expressing herself. Of digesting the world. The more I wrote, the more complete I sounded to myself. The more three-dimensional. Multifaceted. True to life!

And isn't this what all writers dream of? Being so comfortable with words and sentences that they come alive on the page, even if what they are writing is a memo? After all, if you expect to write on a regular basis, either for work or pleasure, it would be alienating to spend day after day with somebody you don't know, who doesn't even seem familiar. To encounter yourself as you write, to feel that you are in synch with yourself, that, as you go about each day, you are not turning your back on yourself, would make life seem rich and attractive.

Looking back, I understand that what helped me begin to reveal myself so fully on the page had everything to do with feeling safe. Safe on so many different levels. I felt safe physically. Walking my laps around the track, with the Berkeley hills rising to the east and the bay spreading to the west, I was at the same time outside, among the sycamores and the squirrels, the sparrows and the jays, and protected from the traffic as well as from wandering off course. Walking around the track, I could never lose my way, take a wrong turn, bump up against a dead end. Yet at the same time I was free—free from decisions about what route to follow, about where to turn and when to stop. When I walked in the neighborhood, or in the Berkeley hills, I had to stay alert—for intersections, cars, unfriendly dogs. And although I didn't need to plan my route ahead of time, I had to be certain I could find my way home.

The conditions that permit a writer to flourish are individual and personal. What works for one or even two or three of us might be all wrong for the next person. It is up to each of us to explore and discover just what it is we want to write. Not what we always thought we were going to write or should write. Not what anybody else—our parents or our teachers—thought we should write. But what, when all is said and done, we feel most natural and comfortable writing. I have known academics who have accumulated lengthy bibliographies of articles in prestigious journals but have great difficulty undertaking book-length manuscripts. When they tell me, "All I've published is articles; it's only right that I try my hand at something longer," I say, "Not necessarily." Deciding to write an academic tome can be an arbitrary decision, one that is not appropriate for all professors. Determining beforehand, in a vacuum, what you should and should not write distances you from your writing and all that you hold most dear. Instead, I urge all writers to provide the most fertile of soil for themselves and then to pay close attention as their words begin to find the page, making certain that what they are writing is appropriate for their particular climate and growing conditions.

Try This

1. Borrow from the library or buy a book of haiku poetry. Spend several hours reading through the poems and thinking about the form—three lines of five, seven, and five syllables each. Once you have familiarized yourself with the genre, set aside fifteen minutes for the next four or five days to write haiku. Don't rush. Let the images and lines come to you as slowly or as quickly as they offer themselves. How did it feel to write poetry instead of what you usually write? Did you feel freer, more relaxed as you wrote?

2. Read a brief collection of short stories by a writer like Raymond Chandler, Eudora Welty, Anton Chekoff, or Lorie Moore. When you have finished, think about the form of the short story, with its spareness, its forward momentum, its single action. If the form appeals to you, create a character and a situation—you can borrow from real life—and try writing a story of your own. What was your experience writing in this new genre? Was it exciting to use your imagination in creating the story?

3. Take an adventure or incident, an encounter or event from your own life that you find interesting or heightening, and tell about it on the page. To do this, imagine first that you are relating the story at a dinner party, then incorporate the details necessary, especially with the descriptions, to compensate for the absence of a live voice doing the narrating.

4. If you are having difficulty writing, take the piece and see what happens if you rewrite it as a different genre. If you are

writing an office memo or a term paper, try making it into a news story. If you are writing a legal brief or annual report, see what happens if you transform it into a short story. Try turning your short story into a poem. As you write, notice how the change of genre feels. Does it make writing a more comfortable process?

5. If you enjoyed any of these alternate forms of writing, think about taking a class from a community college or extension school. You may discover that writing in this other form functions as a universal unblocking agent, or that you have found a kind of writing you prefer engaging in.

13

Practicing Deep Compassion

Once you begin to feel safer in your relationship with writing, you become optimistic. You see that it is possible to sit down and write on a regular basis. And by now you are familiar enough with your writing process that you know how to deal with the inevitable snags and roadblocks you encounter. If one day you find writing slower or more of a struggle than usual, you understand that this is not the beginning of another drought. Rather, it is simply one slow day. Just that and nothing more. If you read over what you have written for several days and feel dissatisfied, you know not to panic; you can revise. You have been at this juncture before and each time have rewritten the pages in question to your satisfaction. In the same way, if you fail to write for a couple of days, instead of berating yourself you know how to give yourself the necessary slack, and you are able to remind yourself that all it takes to begin again is sitting down with the intention of writing. Everything will flow from there.

It is always gratifying when the work I do with writers has brought them to this point. Together, we have slowly but surely rewired their relationship to writing so that seeing or thinking about their computer, their legal pad, or their desk no longer causes a spike of fear. So that the minute the flow of words slows down or the best expression for a certain idea eludes them, they no longer panic. So that, if they get up from their computer or put their writing pad away with a twinge of malaise about that day's productivity, they do not sink into depression.

Now, after weeks or months or perhaps years of struggle, they have the stability and leisure to sit back and begin to examine their relationship with writing to understand what it means to them and asks of them, and to become confident that they and their writing can live a long and companionable life together. So far their work has shifted what was once dysfunctional and impossible into an activity that is both possible and at times even satisfying. But what a shame to stop here, to leave uncharted all the territory on the other side of what is possible. Why limit their discoveries? What if ahead lie serene mountain valleys, or meadows blazing with wildflowers, or jungles that dazzle with the songs and colors of exotic birds? What if, instead of finding writing tolerable, they could eagerly anticipate its company or experience deep happiness in its presence?

The relationship between writers and their writing lies somewhere between the relationship of friends and that of lovers. It is a relationship that varies over time as well as from writer to writer. For blocked writers the relationship becomes clouded with anxiety or fear and often with anger or hatred—fear of the blank page and anger toward the self who is unable to sit down and write. Once this negative connection between the writer and writing has been established, it is difficult to mend. One or two wounding experiences with the page, and we become negatively conditioned. Each ensuing bad encounter reinforces—even increases—the turbulence we feel toward or about writing, until a psychic battle royal is fought every time we are called upon or intend to write.

A great deal of the work I do with writers involves reconditioning this relationship by providing the writer with a continuous series of positive interactions with the page. Often this is a painstaking process. While two negative interactions may be sufficient to sour our relationship with writing, rehabilitation requires hundreds of good experiences, cultivated in many different ways—from thinking small and creating a safe and pleasing writing harbor to speaking kindly to ourselves and learning to recognize and embrace our individual writing process. Once we are infused with a large-enough dose of good feelings about our ability to sit down and write, we can begin to redefine or recast our relationship with the page as a partnership between our writing process and our hopes and dreams. Now is the moment to deepen that relationship, to poke into every nook and cranny, as we observe our own behaviors and responses in this evolving partnership.

I don't remember exactly when I began to consider myself unstuck. Most likely there was no particular moment, no dramatic event when the waters parted, allowing me to pass from the quicksand of writer's block into the terra firma of fluency. No one experience that allowed me to sit down and write whenever, wherever, and whatever I desired. Certainly I can look back and point to milestones: writing in a coffee shop instead of at my desk; writing into memory instead of from my head; realizing that writing is a multistage process instead of a one-shot product. Yet, when I reflect on my transformation from a blocked to an unblocked writer, I experience more of a continuity, an evolution.

Oddly enough, though, I am aware of a particular moment when I realized that, even though I was no longer blocked, I could continue to improve, to oil my relationship with writing so that my engine ran more and more smoothly. Again, as in other pivotal moments in my life, this one involved voices in my head. One morning, as I sat struggling over how best to describe a woman I was profiling for an essay I was writing, the sweetest, kindest person came along to reassure me. *I know description is difficult for you,* the voice whispered. *But don't worry. It doesn't matter if it takes you longer than it takes other writers. Everybody's different. Everybody writes at her own speed. Just because your hands don't fly across the keyboard, it doesn't mean that you're not a writer.*

Although the voice spoke words I had often repeated to myself, this experience was different. As I listened to the voice, I felt myself move into a state of deep relaxation. Unlike the conscious lessons I had taught myself about attitude, these words had risen from within me. They were internal truths, verities that emerged as a result of all the work I had put into writing and overcoming my block. Far from being formulaic, my response reflected a sense of my uniqueness as an individual and a writer. My words were an acknowledgment of my own particular struggle and relationship with writing. Even if it took me longer to write descriptively than other writers I knew, I was a writer nonetheless. Even if I struggled more or longer to pluck the right word from my head and place it onto the page, I was still a writer. Even if my revision process entailed more iterations than those of other writers, I was a writer. What the voice was telling me, repeating over and over and over again, was that I *was* a writer. Whether I was successful or not. Whether I had bad days or not. Had occasional trouble sitting down to write. Lost my way now and then. I was a writer. And whatever peace I had carved out with my writing self, it was holding. Whatever strategies I had devised to keep from becoming blocked again, they continued to work. Whatever style, whatever voice or pace or schedule I had evolved, I was a writer.

To remain unstuck writers must be familiar with, and embrace their writing process from beginning to end. While some writers may feel comfortable with the first draft and struggle with revision, others find revision the more satisfying phase of their process. While some writers may draw the most enjoyment from narrative and description, others find dialogue the most attractive element of their writing. While some writers devote uninterrupted hours or days to writing, others work best in spurts or with frequent intermissions. While some enjoy the stimulation of music while they write, others require silence. What was essential, I realized, if I wanted to keep writing, was that I remain intimate with my process and continue to embrace it. That I allow myself to write within my own time, at my own pace. That I embrace my writing as my own and continue to resist the temptation to compare myself to other writers. This meant that, when I wrote, I would remain fully who I was, writing naturally, from within myself rather than from without. I would no longer, in my initial drafts, play the role of conductor, flourishing my wand to create desired effects. No, I would play from the very center of the orchestra, from a spot that would no longer allow me to distance myself from the other musicians. From this spot, with the notes and phrases washing over and through me, I would play as much in response to the music of the musicians surrounding me as to the written score. I would no longer try to remain in control, to make demands and achieve the mastery I had once pushed myself toward. From now on I would let myself be.

As long as we are blocked as writers, we expend most of our

energy on trying to change everything about the way we write. If we could only sound more sophisticated on the page. More direct. More erudite. If we could only write as fast as we think, sitting erect in a chair in front of our computer, our mind transparent, our thoughts linear, logical. Far from accepting anything about ourselves and our writing, we are convinced that unless we effect dramatic, even wholesale alteration, our writing will never work. Accepting ourselves is the furthest thing from our mind.

Yet it was only once I stopped trying to reengineer everything about my writing and instead accepted my presence on the page that I made any real progress. Certainly, transformation was not at all what I expected when I relinquished my expectations of change; yet transformation was indeed what I experienced. I can explain this best by telling about another discovery, in a completely different realm—an experience I had about two months after I started my year of walking and writing. One day, as I was completing my laps, I realized that I was walking faster and more effortlessly than ever before. I also realized that my speed this day, unlike most others, had nothing to do with a decision on my part. I had not been conscious of wanting to walk faster. Indeed, I had not even thought about speed that morning. And yet there I was, with my pace quickened considerably. How had this come about?

On reflection I realized that my body had, on its own, shifted gears. From first to second and then on to third, I had quickened my pace naturally, moving through the gears without giving it a thought. What is more, since this shift had occurred incrementally, with no conscious intervention on my part, I had increased my speed in total relaxation.

This was different from my usual mode of walking. Most days I observed myself as I walked, at some times conscious of speed, at others of posture, and at still others of the placement of my feet. On those mornings when I judged that I was walking too slowly and decided to walk faster, I would push myself ahead, creating in the process a certain amount of tension within my body. I realized that this tension was counterproductive. It meant that my muscles were perhaps more than optimally contracted. That a portion of my energy was expended, not on walking, but on watching myself move around the track. Speeding up naturally, without obvious volition, meant that my body created no resistance to moving forward in space. Instead of my mind establishing my pace, it was my body that had eased itself into a movement that was in synch with the turgor of my muscles and the elasticity of my limbs at that particular moment.

Although it took longer, I believe something similar happened with my writing. Once I decided to refrain from twisting and turning myself into the kind of writer I aspired to be, I became more and more relaxed and authentic on the page. The extreme resistance I had felt as a blocked writer and then the milder resistance I had created as an aspiring writer fell away. No longer did I hold my breath when I wrote. Or begin to breathe shallowly, through my throat and not my diaphragm, whenever I sat at my computer. Now I could respire fully, a deep breath in and a long breath out, in and out, in and out. And, lo and behold, because I was offering no resistance, words, images, phrases seemed to flow out of me. More and more my writing felt like an extension of myself, my fullest self, the person I was, not only in front of a class teaching or at a dinner party entertaining—my public self—but the Jane Anne who lives with Steve and takes the kind of risks we take with partners and lovers, speaking with full articulation at certain moments and in abbreviation at others. Speaking from her intellect some days, and from her heart and soul much more often. With measured reason some hours and in the heat of passion at others.

A client who had been struggling with her third book announced that she had decided to push herself to the very edge in her writing. She was tired of being afraid and playing it safe. She wanted to put herself on the line, spiritually, emotionally, intellectually, and academically. "I don't like who I am in my first two books," she said. "I want to create a whole new person on the page. And I don't want to be afraid of what my readers will think."

When I looked dubious, she told me that she knew this would work. Years ago, when she had injured her back, she had discovered a form of yoga called Kripalu Yoga, and it helped her recovery more than anything else she tried. "What they do is push you right to the edge of your pain, make you engage in whatever movement causes you to feel the first twinges. And then they teach you that the pain itself isn't as intense as your fear of the pain."

I nodded.

"So that's what I want you to help me do with my writing. I don't want to waste any more time. I want to push myself right into the kinds of material and the sorts of self-disclosure I'm so afraid of now."

"Hmm," I responded.

"You seem dubious," she said.

"I've discovered that pushing yourself too hard as a writer has negative effects. Rather than forcing you to write differently and take risks, it makes you more afraid, heightening any inhibitions around writing you're already incubating."

"But I'm tired of the way I write. And I no longer have any patience with being so afraid," my client answered.

"I understand," I reassured her. "But I think the best way to make discoveries, to blaze new trails with your writing, is to embrace yourself as a writer. To have compassion for your fears and your hesitations."

"A full adult compassion?" my client responded.

"Exactly," I replied.

"Actually, that makes sense to me."

"If you think about it, Kripalu Yoga works paradoxically," I continued. "By bringing you to the edge of your pain, it demonstrates that you have much less to fear than you anticipated, which allows you to relax and begin moving in ways you had been avoiding before the demonstrations."

"I guess you're right," my client nodded. "So instead of whipping myself toward new intellectual and spiritual heights, I have to practice compassion on myself."

"As you said, deep compassion. You need to understand that the way you dream of writing might frighten you for good reason. That the stakes at this moment may simply be too great. And you have to have compassion for your fear. You have to remind yourself that you might have every reason to be afraid, that you're writing in the best way you can for now. To acknowledge to yourself that your writing is full of important ideas and that you are able to articulate them in ways your readers will understand and build upon."

Most of us need assistance with practicing compassion toward ourselves. It has been so long since we've really listened to ourselves, given ourselves a break, that we don't know how to begin or what to think. To help set my clients on the path, I ask them if there is anything they like about their writing. Almost always, since we have by this time been working together for some months at least, they can point to something that pleases them. "I like the way I tend to use 'you' and address the audience," one client told me recently. "It creates a kind of intimacy." "I appreciate the images I manufacture on the page," another said. "I guess I like how earnest I sound," a law student decided. "It's no wonder I'm afraid when I write," an English professor said, sighing, "considering that my dissertation committee told me my thesis wasn't written in the proper academic style. All these years later I keep waiting for the same thing to happen to me again. But now that I think about it, I like the natural quality of my voice." "I'm pleased that I'm writing at all," a recent MBA told me. "For the first few months of my job, I wasn't able to finish a memo."

Such positive observations are a good place to start. They provide a foothold for deepening a writer's relationship with writing. By holding these statements in our minds when we write, instead of bolting we are able to remain emotionally present as we begin to connect with the page, so that the words, ideas, expressions, and feelings can successfully make the journey from our head to the body of the piece we are writing.

After writers begin to tap into this advanced compassion, its practice becomes easier. Instead of groping for affirming responses to our writing, we discover that these responses present themselves automatically. Once this happens, we are more quickly able to believe and absorb what we "hear."

"The other morning when I was writing," a client told me last week, "my better half started patting me on the back. *That's quite an image you've just created,* it complimented me. *Yes, quite an image.*" Another client, a visual artist who is having trouble completing the text of a book she is working on about the birth of her daughter, found herself feeling particularly positive about the kind of mother she is. "I was sitting there writing about the birthday present I made for my daughter when she was a year old, and suddenly I couldn't help but smile. A big grin, actually. 'You know, honey, you're a damned good mother,' I told myself. 'Yes indeed, damned good.'"

This kind of response to oneself as a writer runs deeper than simply developing a positive attitude. The attitude comes first, shaped by substituting positive statements about your abilities as a writer for the negative accusations you have been flinging at yourself whenever you are unable to write. The attitude facilitates sitting down to write and beginning to capture your words on the page. It can even help you complete a story or an essay or a term paper. But attitude alone is not enough. Not for the long haul. For that you need to develop compassion, which arises from a deepening of your relationship with your writing and yourself. Compassion requires more than attitude; it asks complete involvement, a relation of your heart, your mind, and your soul with your writing.

When I was pregnant with Jonah, my friend Joanne was pregnant with her son, Patrick. We had been close before, but now we became intimate, sharing all the important events of our pregnancies. At the first sensations of quickening, she lay on the floor of my living room, pulled up her shirt, and pointed to her abdomen, tuning me into the almost imperceptible quivers of her baby kicking. We attended prenatal classes together. Went shopping for baby clothes. Visited maternity wards. Measured our bellies. We shared so much of our pregnancies that we joked about giving birth to twins. This intimacy tuned me so into Joanne's labor that while her husband, Howard, made tea and toast throughout the night, I became her Lamaze coach, watching and timing her contractions, breathing with her, joking with her, reassuring her, telling her what a great job she was doing.

Because we had experienced so much of our pregnancies together, I felt free to offer Joanne whatever she needed as she lay in her bed in the middle of the night during the intense hours of her labor. I could whisper to her when I felt she would be soothed by calm, rest my hand lightly on her belly when she needed touch. And joke with her about the contortions of her stomach with each contraction when she needed levity.

We need to be able to do the same for ourselves as writers, establishing strong foundations for intimacy and compassion that will last a lifetime, withstanding the kinds of interruptions and challenges that inevitably come our way. Once, when a group of students were sitting and talking with Marvin Bell, our teacher at the University of Iowa Poetry Workshop, he began to reminisce about former students. Some had become well-known poets; others were no longer writing. In the middle of the conversation, he paused, reflecting for a moment, then turned back to the group. "Don't criticize anybody who stops writing," he told us. "And don't think less of them. There is usually a reason they have stopped, and they may return."

Most of the students in the room were passionate writers, early enough in their careers to find not writing unimaginable. I, however, at the time a tentative writer who knew the pangs of writer's block, took solace in what Marvin had said. Looking back, I see that he was asking of us just the sort of compassion and understanding toward other writers that I now ask my clients to invoke toward themselves. I ask you not to judge yourself as a writer. Instead, accept that you *are* a writer. Take pleasure in those moments, or those elements of your writing, that you can appreciate and enjoy. If you lose yourself in your writing for even five minutes, celebrate that interlude. If during a writing session an unexpected idea emerges, applaud that idea. If one day you wander into a new syntax, savor that prose. If during one writing session you encounter a voice you identify with, embrace that voice.

One of my clients, a scholarly physician, has been trying to write a trade book on his area of medicine. He came to see me because he wasn't able to find the right voice, the proper tone, for the book he anticipated writing. "I either sound too academic and am certain I'll alienate my readers, or I sound too facile and I am terrified that I'll alienate any colleague who happens to read my book."

For months this client struggled with his writing, alternating voices, stuffing one chapter full of academic rhetoric and the next with aphorisms. As we worked together, I asked him which one of his two personae he felt more comfortable with. "The truth is, I don't feel comfortable with either. I think I'm somewhere in between. I would say that my patients find me a very humane, likable, informed guy."

"Sounds good to me," I responded. "As you write over the next two weeks, why don't you notice if that guy ever appears on the page."

Two weeks later he burst into my office. "I had the most wonderful writing experience last week. Something you said took hold, and suddenly I had a lot of compassion for myself and my struggle with writing. The same sort of compassion I have for my patients and their struggle toward health. When I started writing, I felt as if I connected both to myself and to my patients. And voilà, I wrote the first paragraph and was so pleased with my voice, I was on a roll. I wrote some more. After two hours I had written five pages, and the writing has never, ever, felt so effortless for me."

Another client, an academic who had struggled with writing for nearly a decade, beginning articles then abandoning them midway, realized one day that every perspective he adopted was contrarian. "No wonder I've had so much difficulty completing anything I begin. I'm asking for trouble."

"I wonder," I replied, "why you so consistently take the contrarian perspective."

"Maybe I just like to make things difficult for myself," he answered. But several weeks later he told me that he was beginning to have a different view of himself as a writer. "I realized last week that a contrarian is what I am. I tend to see the world a little differently than my colleagues, and this gives me an opportunity both to establish a niche for myself and to tease the rest of my department a little bit. Once I realized this, I was able to appreciate my writing more. Of course it's difficult. I'm going against the current. But it gives me room to inject wit and even humor into my writing, and that's what I'm all about."

It is difficult for any of us to go fully out into the world if we are always second-guessing ourselves, questioning our motives, our decisions, our moral fiber. In the same way, it is difficult to write if we rein ourselves in or hold ourselves back. If we pester ourselves about our voice, about who we are on the page. We must give ourselves permission to write—full, unequivocal permission, no ifs, ands, or buts thrown in for good measure. It is a permission that begins on the surface, with our first layer of skin, but it must penetrate deep into us, to the very core of our lives.

Several years ago a graduate student who was unable even to begin working on her dissertation realized that the topic she was writing about involved a great deal of personal struggle. "I thought my interest in this area was strictly intellectual," she told me. "But last week I realized how emotional I felt about my findings."

"That's not unusual," I told her. "I've found that many students, particularly those in the social sciences, select dissertation topics in areas that cause havoc in their lives. I had a friend who decided to write his dissertation on Decision Theory. What he didn't realize at the time was that he was known in the department as somebody who could never make any decisions about his own life. And another friend, who in his private life was intensely controlling and perfectionistic, wrote about diffuse power in organizations."

It wasn't long after this conversation that the graduate student began to find writing more pleasurable. She had already worked toward sitting down for at least an hour a day to write and was making progress, but now she began to look forward to her writing sessions, which gradually lengthened without her forcing herself to continue writing.

"You know, I think realizing that I was myself struggling with the same issues I was researching and writing about helped me appreciate myself more," she told me one day. "I realized that my own vulnerability helped me feel much more compassion toward the struggles of my research subjects, and I like that about myself. I don't think I'd ever want to lose it."

What develops from cultivating our deep compassion toward ourselves is intimacy with our writing, which allows us to feel both at ease and energized when we write. Sitting down in front of our computer or with our pad and pen in hand, we are with our closest friend—not expected to be on our best behavior, appreciated and understood in all our complexities and contradictions, our darkness as well as our light, in times of distress and in times of fortune, at moments of emptiness and during bursts of inspiration.

Try This

1. Once a week, either before or after you have written, spend some time thinking about what you like about the way you write. Do you like the personality of your narrator on the page? Are you impressed with your vocabulary? Do you appreciate the way your sentences flow? Your images and metaphors? Your directness? Your spareness? Your humor? Your wisdom? Your playfulness? Once you have isolated one or more elements of your writing that you appreciate, remind yourself of these from time to time as you write.

2. Take stock of the way you have been writing this past week. Notice any ways that this is different from the way you wrote in the past. Is it easier to sit down and begin? Do you feel less compelled to revise? Have metaphors begun creeping onto the page? Whatever progress you discover, simply note it and allow yourself to feel grateful for the changes.

3. If there are still areas of writing that feel difficult, make note of them. But instead of becoming angry at yourself, practice compassion. Tell yourself, "It's hard to write so slowly, I know. But at least you are writing." Or, "I know you want to write more figuratively, but notice your humor." Or, "I know you still feel anxious when you write, but look how much you've accomplished in the past month in spite of anxiety."

4. When you are writing, imagine you are a coach helping a tennis player win an important match. In the same way that you would encourage your athlete, offering both reassurance

and tips on strategy, encourage yourself as a writer. Remember, your goal is to help the player feel enough on top of the game to win.

5. If you discover that you are becoming angry or frustrated with yourself when you write, stop writing for a minute and think of one of your closest friends. Imagine she has just told you she is having trouble at work. What would you say to comfort her, to help her work through the anger and disappointment she feels? Now repeat these words to yourself.

14

What's at Stake

"My life seems so different now," a client reflected the other day. "I can't believe I spent so many years struggling with my writing. You know," he continued, "I realize now that that struggle became the focus of my life. What a difference it makes not to feel dread every time I have a memorandum to send out."

Another client, who had just completed her master's thesis after a four-year struggle, felt so confident about her writing future that she enrolled in a nonfiction writing course. "I feel committed to really making this writing thing work," she told me.

Yet another client, in a burst of enthusiasm, volunteered to write her church's newsletter once a month. "I'm so grateful to feel comfortable writing that I wanted to celebrate through service to my congregation," she told me.

Seeing writers once wrought with tension and despair now so upbeat, so optimistic about their writing, used to make me feel elated enough to stand up and dance. What a wonder to witness the transformation of agony into euphoria. Let's celebrate! But now my response is more tempered. I sit back for a moment and smile, joining in the collective sigh of relief. But I no longer feel inclined to rise out of my chair and jig. I know that the recovery is not yet complete: This joy, this elation is not the end of the road. Rather, it is one more stage in the journey from blocked to fluent writer. These clients have indeed covered many miles. But they have not yet had time to appreciate and absorb all they have experienced. They know what sights they have seen but are not yet aware of the deepest meaning of these sights. It is time for their travels to take a different turn, time to slow down, to begin to journey inward, toward the emotional center of their previous block. It's as if they've gone to India and seen the Taj Mahal from the outside but have not yet penetrated its interior. Haven't walked through the gates and heard the echo of their footsteps, seen the exquisite dappled light, the ninety-nine names of Allah written in calligraphy along the top of the tomb.

"Now that you have your bearings and know how you will make the return trip home, let's try to figure out what was at stake for you at the time you had so much difficulty writing," I suggest. I say this because in the past clients I *thought* I had worked with successfully, clients I was certain would continue writing fluently and enthusiastically on their own, called me up in despair, sometimes months after our last meeting, sometimes years. To varying degrees and in various ways, they told me the same thing: I'm back where I started. I can't write a word. In fact, some of these writers felt even worse than when they first came to see me. They had thought they were cured, but they had once again come down with the same symptoms. Now it felt like there was truly no hope.

When the first recidivists phoned, I was shaken. What had gone wrong? Where had I failed? Why hadn't I realized there was more work to be done? And I was angry with myself. It was all my fault; I had caused people who had already suffered to suffer again. Thinking I had helped them was arrogant!

Once I was able to calm down and reflect, I realized that all

was not lost. I still had one very successful specimen before me—
a specimen I could study to figure out where I had gone wrong
with my clients and how I might help them recover their equilib-
rium. After all, I had learned most of what I knew from reflecting
on my own writing block and recovery. What I needed to do
now was to take a closer look, particularly at the past several years,
when, more and more, writing had become a natural and essential
part of my life. When my day felt whole only if I had spent time
writing. When after many years I could finally tell people that I
was a writer without taking a deep breath or crossing my fingers
or feeling a quiver of insincerity.

This is the kind of reflection all blocked writers, if we want to
ensure our future writing fluidity, must at some time engage in.
But we must not turn in this direction too early in our journey.
To dive deep into these emotional waters, we must be certain of
our ability to swim—to lift our arms, kick our legs, and breathe
every few strokes—as we begin to accumulate distance. Thinking
too hard before we have mastered the fundamentals interferes
with this process, when more than anything what we need is to
master the mechanics of finding a time and a space to write and
doing what we can to make this time and this space safe. Swimming, we would not venture out near sharks or in a strong under-
tow. Writing, we learn to ask our critics to leave, and to invite our
supporters in. Some of us may explore how comfortable we feel
with the genre we have been writing in. We may shift our focus
to a more appreciative audience. We may even begin to think
back to any positive writing experiences we may have forgotten.
Only once we are swimming freely should we dive in deeper and
ask ourselves what might have caused our block in the first place.

Trying to fathom what had gone wrong for my clients, I asked myself, again and again, what had shifted for me? What had been necessary for me to truly *feel* like a writer? I knew that it wasn't simply being able to sit down and write once again, although that had been a pivotal part of the process. Something more had been necessary to complete the transformation, to allow writing to penetrate all the levels of my existence, something that had enabled me not only to become unblocked but to open myself, pore by pore, to the act of writing. What was that something, that final ingredient that had turned me from somebody who could write into a writer through and through?

To overcome writing block our first energies are necessarily directed at behaving "as if." On the inside we are troubled about writing, anxious about the process as well as the outcome. And because many of us have already grasped at stopgap measures and quick-and-easy cures, we are now realistic enough to understand that working through our block will take time. But we have to begin somewhere, so we start by thinking small, by limiting our goals and our writing time, by noticing the chorus of critics within us and quieting them. Over time we are more and more able to look like writers. We can sit down to write on a regular basis. We can complete projects. We can even talk about our writing. But so far, even though we have traveled many miles, we have only managed to change our behavior. We haven't yet undergone the transformation that will allow us to feel like writers through and through, from the inside out.

When I considered my recent writing life—showing up and writing every day for at least two hours, ignoring the distractions that in the past had kept me from the page—I realized that what had changed was the way I understood and perceived the causes and consequences of my writing block. I had finally grasped the deepest sources of this struggle, had seen how events and emotions had converged when I was in college to make it almost impossible for me to write.

To reach this understanding I had had to put on a headlamp and peer into my previous block, layer by layer, until I had visited all the sites that had contributed to my paralysis. This was a journey in depth rather than in breadth, a journey down into the center of my fear rather than around its perimeter. A journey that forced me to become saturated with the sounds, smells, and textures I encountered. This was not a voyage of the intellect only. It was a journey that required the participation of the heart and soul. When I set out, I knew the face, the surface of my block, but I was ignorant of its interior. When I returned, I had explored its every recess. And I knew as well that, at last, there was nothing to be afraid of.

That is why I now tell blocked writers who have traveled far enough to indulge in optimism about their writing that their journey is not yet complete. That now it is time to revisit the darkness of their past block, in order to protect their return to the light. Some writers are eager to set out on this second trek, anxious to know as much as they can learn about their relationship with writing. Others are understandably hesitant, reluctant to risk additional pain or hardship when it seems to them they have already accomplished their goal. "If I know what to do when I'm feeling anxious about my writing," a client said recently, "why can't I just keep doing what you've taught me so far? It obviously works. Why should I mess with a good thing?"

I explain that writing block is a symptom of fear or a reaction to powerful anxiety, and that, until we become familiar with that fear or anxiety, we are not free to continue writing with success.

If what we are afraid of remains a mystery, it can still wield power over us.

"Think about one of your patients," I suggested to my client who is a well-known doctor in the area. "If someone came to you with an intractable fever, and over the course of several months of tests and medication, you managed to eliminate the fever but were unable to discover its etiology, would you feel confident that the patient would continue to remain fever free?"

"No," he responded. "If I didn't know the cause or the origin of the fever, I wouldn't know why it had disappeared. And if I didn't know why it had disappeared, I would worry about a recurrence."

"Exactly," I said. "So, if we consider your writing block a fever, all we've accomplished is to make it disappear. But we still don't know why you were suffering from the fever in the first place. That's the work I want to do with you now. The final step in establishing total fluency on the page is to fathom just what you used to be—and most likely still are—afraid of."

"That's easy," the doctor responded. "I was—and I think I still am—afraid of failing. Isn't that what everybody's block is all about?"

Fear of failure is a concept we all know, both through personal experience and pop psychology. For every bright kid who performs below his ability in school, for every artistic soul who fails to create art, for every athlete whose performance disappoints, how often we hear that, rather than risk failure they have simply not tried. I used to think something similar about myself. "I hate to compete," I insisted to friends and family. And when I said this, I meant that I couldn't bear the possibility of coming up short. Rather than risk being "less than," I simply took myself out of the arena of competition.

Some blocked writers experience this fear of failure concretely. "Whenever I sit down to work on my dissertation," a graduate student told me, "I can almost see and hear my committee gathered around the table at my defense, telling me that my work simply doesn't deserve to pass. The scene is so real that I feel humiliation rising like heat from my toes to the top of my head. Sometimes I even break out in a sweat."

An assistant professor who had suffered a nervous depression after completing his tenure article kept imagining the chairman of his department telling him that instead of working toward tenure he should check himself into the local psychiatric hospital. "You're never going to make it," the chairman would say. "You're just not stable enough."

To a certain extent the fear-of-failure explanation is justified. Just about every one of us can point to at least one particularly humiliating failure. "My editor rejected the first half of my book," a poet told me. "Of course, I'm terrified of that happening again." "My senior year of high school my English teacher told me I was one of the worst writers she had ever had," a successful lawyer confessed recently. "Ever since then I've been afraid somebody was going to attack my writing in the same way again." "When I was growing up," a CEO confided to me, "I was never as smart as my brother. And my father let me know this all the time. I think now, every time I have to write, I'm afraid somebody will say the same thing, tell me I'm just not smart enough." "My mother has always read everything I write. Several years ago she told me my latest script was trite," a young screenwriter told me. "Now, even though I understand that her comment had less to do with my writing than with her recent divorce from my father, I'm worried that one of my readers will say the same thing."

When I first began working with blocked writers, what surprised me was not that so many of them could point to certain moments in the past when something they wrote had been criticized. After my first five clients such an event was easy to predict. No, what seemed curious to me was that for every blocked writer these events or moments continued to stand out, despite previous and subsequent success. The woman whose publisher had sent the first half of her book back for revision had won prestigious fellowships as a graduate student, had written a successful dissertation, and had recently published a collection of poems that was well received by the public. The lawyer had become a prominent litigator, known for the clarity and cogency of his briefs. The CEO whose father had found him wanting compared to his older brother had become nationally prominent. And the screenwriter had recently won two prestigious screen-writing awards. Despite these noteworthy successes each of them seemed to cling to one or two moments of disappointment or humiliation from the past concerning their writing, instantly recalling these moments when the flow of words onto the page slowed down or stopped. Why, I wondered, did these failures so easily push their way onto center stage? Why are blocked writers not able to understand that their worry about failure is most likely not well-founded? Why do they return again and again to an isolated moment in their lives? Indeed, why can't they see that the criticism they so fear is the opinion of a very small minority, an anomaly even, in a life or career where their peers have generally voiced approval and praise? In other words, why does one negative moment seem to cancel out a succession of positive experiences?

Of course, not all writers' biographies are so clear. My father had a great deal of support for his view of my writing from my college professors. Whether or not I imagined or exaggerated my father's criticism of my personal essay, the comments on my term papers throughout my freshman year reinforced his view and confirmed my fears. Another of my clients had a similar experience. His mother was an English teacher, and nothing her son ever wrote seemed to satisfy her. "Either it was my word choice or my punctuation or my spelling or my organization she shook her head over. No matter how hard I worked, how much I revised, she was always disappointed in me. And worried about what my teachers would think of her for having a child who wrote so poorly."

"No wonder you became a blocked writer," I said.

"Yes," my client answered. "Then when I went to college, I worked hard on my writing hoping that my professors would praise me. I worked to make my mother happy."

"Did they?" I asked.

"I didn't think so at the time. But later, I realized that every once in a while, they did have something nice to say about my style."

It was this client's comment that sent me back to my years in college and the intensifying of my own writing block. It was then that I remembered the high-school journalism award I had won. Whereas previously I had always taken for granted that any feedback I received about my writing had been negative, now I was forced to see my block in a different light. After all, nobody had helped me write my articles for our high-school newspaper. In fact, I had joined the staff my senior year, not my junior year, after much of the training for the reporters had taken place. As a writer for the *Merionite*, I had been on my own, required to figure out the rules and conventions of journalism, responsible only to my readers and not to any higher power. What is more, all those years later I remembered feeling proud of myself for my *Merionite* success and concluding that at least in this way I resembled my brilliant father, who had intended to become a journalist before he had changed courses to study physics. In fact, the more I thought back to my senior year in high school and my afternoons spent in the *Merionite* office writing and editing, the more clearly I remembered hearing about my father as not only a brilliant scientist but a gifted writer as well.

What had happened? Why had my father's apparent criticism of my college essay obliterated all the positive associations with writing I had formed during my senior year? Why had the voices of the newspaper editor and adviser, of my friends and the subjects of my features, become silent? And, conversely, why were the comments of my professors, who found my writing lacking, so quickly able to fill my head? Why had I become so helpless, unable to answer back, to defend myself?

Such questions are among the most important that blocked writers can ask themselves. Once we have realized that fear of failure might be too easy an explanation for all of our struggles around writing, and once we are confident that we are no longer completely blocked, we may begin to wonder how we allowed this to happen. Why we didn't allow any of the compliments, any of the reinforcement, to penetrate. Why we were so easily convinced by criticism, so quick to turn against ourselves.

My client had begun to ask himself these questions. Why was his mother's voice the only one he heard throughout college? Why, in spite of proof that his mother was not always right in her strong criticism of his writing, did he still seem to accept her opinion as valid? Why, no matter how he strained to negate his mother's power over him, to contradict what she said, was he not able to write?

For every blocked writer a similar contradiction lurks in the wings. Why, despite evidence to the contrary, do the academics and executives, the writers and lawyers and graduate students who become blocked persist in believing that they cannot write? Certainly, most of my clients have experienced success, academic and often professional as well. With so much data to the contrary, why is every client I have ever worked with so confident that they will fail? That, by beginning or completing or submitting their manuscript, their memo, their brief, their ineptness, their stupidity, their incompetence will be exposed? Indeed, that whatever is wrong or lacking in them will not only be revealed, but their lives will unravel, bit by bit, dollar by dollar, friend by friend, colleague by colleague?

Fear of failure certainly plagues every blocked writer I have worked with. But I knew it could only be half the truth. Despite the fear of shame and humiliation, there had to be more. What lies behind the nightmares and imagined disasters blocked writers report? What accounts for the psychologist who dreams of being chased by the senior members of his department through the halls of the university where he teaches? Where has the executive gathered material for the dramas she imagines when she has to write a year-end summary of her company's transactions—dramas complete with scenes of her fleeing from a meeting?

And what was I so frightened of those long nights I sat awake during college, typing away, the floor about me littered with sheets of paper? How could I have become so terrified that each sentence felt menacing enough for me to rewrite it again and again and again?

Something wasn't making sense. Failure itself was not as monstrous as were these fears. I knew undergraduates who rewrote papers to improve their grades. Graduate students who had reworked their entire dissertation and continued on to fine academic careers. I knew people who had lost their jobs. Certainly they had been upset, but they were not as shaken as blocked writers who, whenever they think about writing, *anticipate* failure.

Something else must be driving the fear so many blocked writers express. Something we all share yet are equally unconscious of. A danger even more real and threatening than writing that doesn't quite make the grade. A danger that disguises itself, masquerading in the costume of fear of failure. What could we be facing, unconsciously, that deep down feels even worse than failure? More frightening than having to revise our term paper, even our doctoral dissertation? Than our boss asking us to rewrite a memo? What, I asked myself over and over again, could possibly be lurking down in the briny depths of our writing block?

It is not easy to suggest to blocked writers that it isn't failure that so many of them fear most. Many of them work hard to convince themselves that they have enough food to feed this particular monster for years to come. To suggest that it isn't failure that stands between them and their writing is outrageous. Faced with such resistance, I quickly saw that for me to push too hard against fear of failure with my clients was counterproductive. And since so many of them seemed determined to hold on to the possibility of not being good enough, I began to see that this fear, this terror of humiliating ourselves, might be serving a purpose. Perhaps, paradoxically, focusing on the fear of failure creates a safety net for blocked writers. Perhaps it is the only way we can make sense of our persistent block, the only way we can release our-

selves from the charges of "lazy," "undisciplined," "disorganized"
we have for so long been hurling at ourselves.

Unable to convince my clients prematurely of a different possibility, I came to understand that believing that they might
indeed fall short was another stage in the process of overcoming
writing block. When they first came to see me, these writers were
so intent on *not* letting themselves off the hook, they couldn't
even consider the emotional sea they were tossing upon. No, it
wasn't a question of what they felt, each of them insisted. It was
laziness, or lack of discipline or disorganization, that made it
impossible for them to write. If they just couldn't get it together
the way other writers did, it was because they weren't as good as
others, were morally inferior in fact. Once we had worked
together long enough for them to understand that, no, they
weren't stupid or lazy, they were able to consider that their block
might have an emotional core. Perhaps there was a reason they
could not write. A good reason. Perhaps they were afraid of failing.

This is a crucial insight. Believing that there is genuinely
something at stake, something as horrendous as failure, allows
blocked writers to relax the noose they have been holding around
their necks. After all, if there really is something to be afraid of,
not being able to write makes sense. And if we believe we are
really afraid of failing, we can begin to see ourselves in a new
light. Instead of being angry, we can feel compassion for our
struggle. Instead of submitting to the stern schoolmarm or the
rigid sergeant barking out orders, motivating by command, chastisement, and punishment, we can become gentle with ourselves,
feel the first twinges of empathy, inspire ourselves to write
through understanding.

I began to realize that, before writers can begin to release
themselves from their fear of failure, they have to experience a

prolonged honeymoon with themselves and their writing. They have to feel unblocked and comfortable long enough for their fear of failure to begin loosening its grip. They need to encounter a period of success, a succession of weeks or months when the fear of failure doesn't flicker across their mental screen. When they can begin to see that writing isn't all that difficult. That something else must have been stirring up the anguish about sitting down to write.

It is at this point, once blocked writers feel secure enough to relinquish their fear of failure, that I suggest that perhaps, just perhaps, this fear is not the real culprit. That it never has been. That what almost all writers struggling to sit down and translate their ideas into words—almost all writers who cannot write—are afraid of is just the opposite of failure. What they are terrified of is success. Yes, success. They are afraid of writing and completing their writing projects because in their inner world success may bring nasty consequences in its wake.

Of course, it is nearly impossible to know this on our own. Being afraid of success flies in the face of the culture we live in. How, when our schools, our families, our entire advertising industry promulgate getting ahead, generational upward mobility, keeping up with the Joneses, the Chus, and the Martinezes, can we be afraid to succeed?

Or, if it doesn't sound like the most outrageous of contradictions, being afraid of success has the resonance of a cliché, a psychological aphorism with a New Age twist. That's right, take the responsibility away from the individual, erase the possibility that our failure is in any way our fault, tell us that the problem is not that we are not good enough. That instead we might be too good.

Yet this is indeed what I have come to believe: many blocked writers are unable to write because without being aware of it they are afraid of writing too well. As contradictory or paradoxical as this appears, again and again my clients have led me to this truth.

A lawyer I worked with, who had been one of the top students in a prestigious law school and was so successful during his first few years of practice that he was put up for partnership provides a clear example. He had excelled at the private high school he attended, was accepted at Yale as an undergraduate, and went on to study at Oxford. But now he had difficulty completing briefs for important cases. At first his "by the time I've written the first eight-to-ten pages, I've convinced myself that what I'm writing just isn't very important, that nobody will believe what I'm saying," convinced me. After all, his anxiety seemed plausible. I'd heard it before, so it must be true. But then I realized that, for many years of his life, he didn't experience this difficulty in completing what he began. Quite the opposite. The reason he landed his position at a prestigious law firm in the first place was his many accomplishments. What is more, he told me that he had a reputation for the lucidity of the memoranda he sent to the various members of his team. Then, with some more probing, I discovered that as an undergraduate he had written speeches for a nationally prominent senator.

There is also my own history, which is certainly not as stellar as that of many of my clients. Merely a staff member of my high-school paper, I wasn't even all that outstanding as a high-school student. But I was certainly not a failure either. I graduated with a 3.5 average, seventeenth in a class of two thousand, with SAT scores just below 1400, and I was accepted at a collection of fine

East Coast schools. Yet, by the time I sat down to write my first term paper for my world history class as a freshman in college, I felt stupid and inarticulate, unable to gather enough words on the page to complete two sentences before I wanted to throw my arms up in despair. And over the next four years my professors did indeed conspire to make me worry about failing each time I turned a paper in to be read and graded.

I, of all people, know how easily and intensely we can be terrified of failure each time we sit down to write. So how did I begin to see the playing field from a new perspective? From thinking of myself as thrown to the lions each time I sat down to write, how did I come to realize that I was on the other side, among the onlookers, vulnerable only because I might just be responsible for the destruction of the prisoner condemned to fight the cuts snarling and flailing at him in the arena below me?

The climax took place one night several years ago, when my parents and brother were visiting me in Berkeley. We went out for a fine dinner and were lingering over dessert when the subject of politics arose. Because my father was more conservative than me, I usually steered clear of such discussions. But that night I jumped in, eager to defend my position and display my knowledge. I no longer remember the precise topic, only that it was a subject I had given thought to around the time of the visit and considered important enough to pursue. Perhaps my own passionate conviction caused me to make my case too aggressively. Maybe I was uncomfortable going up against my father, and my discomfort led me to argue too vociferously.

"You've become a snob," my father hissed at me. "I never thought my daughter would become a snob." And then he leaned forward and stared. Only his usually soft brown eyes spoke to me through his glare. Silence. More silence. Overwhelmed by the intensity of my father's reaction, I was unable to respond. I sat there, tension mounting within me, until, no longer able to contain the geyser that threatened to erupt, I burst into tears and ran outside. *He hates me, he hates me, he hates me,* was all I could think, my body prickled with fear. And then the sobs broke forth, wave after wave, as I paced around and around the block.

To fully understand what happened that night in the restaurant would take years. Perhaps it is only now, as I write this chapter, that the skein of emotions aroused at that table can completely unravel, leaving me with one very long strand to follow back far enough into the past that I can finally understand the dynamic that held me bound so tightly in its thrall that I was unable to express myself on the page.

As a child, I was aware of a stain of unhappiness within my father that darkened even his brightest moments. Something had gone wrong at his dissertation defense—this much I thought I knew—and I attributed all of my father's discomfort to this. I understood that because of anti-Semitism he had been forced to rewrite his Ph.D. dissertation and as a consequence receive his degree from a less-prestigious university than the one where he had begun his graduate career. In my young mind this was a life-long source of unhappiness for my father. I had another factoid as well. The other bit of information I had about my father's past was his excellence as a writer and his original and early desire to become a journalist. He had been editor-in-chief of his high-school newspaper and had chosen the college he attended because it had an excellent journalism program.

My father's unhappiness with the course of his graduate career and his early love of journalism and writing were realities disconnected from my father's life with me. Where my own story and personality enter the drama is the way I combined those two "facts" to create a role for myself as my father's protector, a presence to distract him from any unhappiness. This was not a role of which I was conscious until quite recently. If you had asked me, I would have portrayed a very different situation. My father was my hero. He was smarter and funnier than any other father I knew; anything that was wrong he could right.

This was the ticker-tape story. Much deeper within me, beyond the reach of my conscious mind, the roles were reversed. In this theater my poor father had been wronged. The professors on his dissertation committee had violated his brilliance and ruined his life. Now his days were spent in misery, circling around his decision to jump the journalism ship and strike out for physics. *If only,* I imagined him thinking again and again, *if only I had stayed with journalism, become a writer as I had planned, none of this would have happened.*

This is where my role as protector came in. It was up to me to keep my father from feeling bad, shamed by his dissertation failure, regretful that he had not stuck with journalism. All the ways I tried to make my father proud of me, from working furiously to be elected to Phi Beta Kappa in college to speaking fluent French, were part of my enacting this role. But the collection of strategies I employed to ease what I had decided was my father's pain is not as important for my story as my realizing that my writing block was not a failure of writing ability on my part. Instead, it was one of the means I invented, albeit completely without my own knowledge—or anybody else's—to protect my father from his unhappiness. Excelling in French, election to Phi Beta Kappa—these honors would make my father proud and in no way remind him of his disappointment with himself. But writing! Now that could be lethal. If I continued to be recognized for my ability to express myself on the page, my father might become despondent about having left his career in journalism. And none of us—not my father, not my mother, nor my brother nor I—would survive such a state of affairs.

This is the plot I began to perceive that evening after I fled sobbing from the restaurant. It is a plot based on two bits of information about my father that I received as a child. Two bits of information I combined with my own projections and imagination over the years until I came to believe that it was up to me to keep my father, an internationally known physicist who now has an observatory named after him at the South Pole, from being consumed by shame and regret.

I no longer know if it was that same evening of our restaurant confrontation or later that I understood my father's response to the vehemence of my argument against his view. What I thought was anger was actually the shock of betrayal. Although he was in no way responsible for the role I carved for myself in his life, I think my father had come to expect my allegiance and enthusiastic support. Had come to assume our views would coincide. Now, for the first time in forty-odd years, I was saying, "No. No, I don't agree with you. No, I think you're wrong. Dead wrong!" It must have felt as if I were pointing a gun at his temple!

My clients' stories are every bit as moving as mine. The brilliant lawyer who has difficulty completing the articles he hopes to publish regards his father, a nationally known and celebrated attorney, with reverence. For years he thought his block was provoked by a fear of not living up to his father's genius. Now he sees that his stack of incompletes is a consequence of a terrible scandal his father was involved in many years ago. In my client's view the scandal undermines his father's happiness as well as his reputation. By holding himself back my client suffers along with his father rather than surpassing him.

Several years ago, I worked with a graduate student who couldn't imagine that she would be smart enough to earn her doctorate—even though she had received grant after grant to fund her research, as well as the commendations of many professors in her department. When she finally was able to complete her thesis, her parents came from the Midwest to attend the graduation ceremony. "You're so lucky," her mother said to her after the processional. "With a Ph.D. in hand you'll never be stuck living in a redneck town the way I have been." It was this chance— or was it chance?—remark of her mother's that helped my client see what had kept her from moving ahead with her graduate work for so many years. A graduate of Welseley College, her mother had at one time shown great promise as a biologist. But instead of pursuing a career, as few women of her generation did, my client's mother had married a man who had returned to the Midwest to assume the reins of the family business. While she was blocked, my client believed unconsciously that, if she finished her Ph.D. program, her mother would be reminded of the loss of her youth and promise. By turning her dissertation into the graduate committee, she would be leaving her mother behind.

Usually the roots of writing block travel deep, all the way back to our lives as children in our nuclear family. But this doesn't mean that we have to look that far back in order to bump up against someone our success might harm. I've worked with women whose partners are less educated or less successful than they are. Somewhere on their itinerary these women begin to realize that they are afraid their success will interfere with their relationship: that their partner will leave them or resent them or feel so terrible about their own inadequacies that they will no longer be able to function. I have worked with a woman who accumulated quite a collection of short stories but was unable to submit any of them for publication. The mother of three young children, she told me she was terrified she would lose her lifelong hope of becoming a writer if editors rejected her stories. "What if I send out some of my pieces and can't get them accepted anywhere? I'll be left with no hope. All I'll be is a suburban mother with three young children." While rejection by publishers can indeed be devastating, it turned out that my client had a deeper terror: If she became a successful writer, what kind of mother would she be for her children? In her mind being a good writer and being a good mother were incompatible.

In stating that a fear of success very often lies at the root of writing block, I don't mean to imply that our parents, our siblings, our mates—even our children—are responsible for our inability to write. Very often it is the writers themselves, with their unusually keen sensitivity and intuition, who build their own emotional traps. And when they first try to overcome their blocks, they seem to fear that they will be forced to gnaw a leg or arm off in order to free themselves to write.

But, as I have experienced both in my own life and with my clients, the process of returning to our words, to our voices, to ourselves in no way involves violence. Quite the opposite. The violence is all located at the other end of the journey, even before we set out, when as blocked writers we live in a perpetual state of anger with ourselves. This violence begins to dissipate once we take the first steps along the path to fluency. The journey we embark on is a gentle one, taken at our own speed, one small step at a time. Instead of involving harm and contortions, it is a journey that calls upon compassion—a compassion that can be

invoked not only toward ourselves, but also toward those we most
fear will suffer harm if we free ourselves from our block.

The latest chapter in my own story has my father writing a book
about his career as a physicist. The two of us meet every few
weeks to discuss what he is writing. One afternoon I listened to
what my father had to say about a class he took as a freshman,
titled General Physics, where he discovered his passion for this
new science. Listening to him, I felt shivers of excitement. When
he told me that he originally thought he would specialize in medical physics, and only in graduate school fell in love with cosmic
rays, I heard myself—body, mind, and spirit—utter the deepest
sigh of relief.

So this is my father's story. He fell in love with physics. Is still
in love. And he's saying nothing about regretting leaving journalism behind. In fact, he thinks the two fields are similar, both calling for exploration, independence, sleuthing, and love of
adventure. And as he talks, his eyes come alive, absorbing and
reflecting the afternoon light entering my office through the wall
of French doors behind him. At last! After all these years, this is
my father's story. I can sit back and let him tell it to me—and to
the world—as he actually lived it!

As for me, before I could experience the pleasure of these
afternoons with my father, I had to be able to sit down and write.
To take pleasure in my own words, my own voice, in what I had
to say and the way I had to say it. I had my first taste of this pleasure when, as a professor of French at a small Midwestern college,
I began once again to write the poetry I had abandoned years
earlier. Over the next twenty years this pleasure became more and
more intense as I fashioned a new relationship with my writing.
It is a relationship built upon trust. A relationship that allows me

to talk to myself as my own best friend when I write. That reminds me to think small. To fashion a personal writing process tailored to me, to my own peculiar pace and rhythm, to my own abilities—and deficits as well. It is a relationship built, above all, upon compassion. For without compassion, both for ourselves and for our loved ones, how can we not be afraid to pluck words and ideas from deep within us and expose them on the page? Without compassion how can we trust our own eyes, not to mention the eyes of the world, to read our naked words, their skin so thin that you can follow the veins leading to our heart? Without compassion how can we hope that the words we put on page after page will be received in the world—and heard?

Try This

1. Imagine that you have completed your dissertation, that you have even defended it and passed the defense with flying colors. Or imagine that you have not only written the brief for the biggest case you have ever defended but have gone to court and won the case. Or imagine that your collection of stories has been accepted and published, and has received rave reviews. Or imagine that you have completed your report, and because of what you wrote, your department has been reconfigured, and you have received a promotion. How do you feel about your success? What about your friends? Your family? Is everyone thrilled for you? Are a few not so thrilled?

2. If you imagine any of your friends and family reacting negatively to your success, can you explain their reaction? Why might they be unhappy instead of pleased? What effect might your success have on their lives?

3. If upon reflection you feel that someone you know might be threatened by your success, check in with yourself to see if all of your information is accurate. If you are not certain about your facts, try to discover the truth. Will your younger brother really be unhappy if you finish your dissertation, or is this a story left over from your childhood? Even though your mother has always wanted to be a writer and has never published, will she really be unhappy if you succeed? If you write a stellar brief and win your case, will your partner really feel envious, or are you just worried that she will?

4. If you decide that a friend or family member will actually be unhappy about your success, think about how you can honor this truth and his or her feelings while at the same time continuing to support your relationship to writing. Acknowledge your loved one's feelings and reaction while reminding yourself not to turn your back on your writing, not to abandon this relationship you have worked so hard to improve, sustain, and nourish in spite of your fears and anxieties.